Senior's Guide Book Samsung Galaxy S20, Plus and Ultra

Master Your Device with Expert Tips and Tricks

Nobert Young

TABLE OF CONTENT

Introduction 9

The Layout of the Samsung S20 Series........................... 10

Chapter 1: Getting Started/ Unboxing the Samsung S20 13

SIM Installation 13

How to Set up the Samsung Galaxy S20 Series 13

Power On Your Device 18

Switch Off Your Device 18

Restart Your Device....................................... 19

Auto- Restart Your Device................................. 19

Double Tap to Wake Up 20

Lift to Wake Feature...................................... 21

Force-close Apps 22

Status Icons 23

Setup Samsung Backup..................................... 24

Chapter 2: Side Key Settings 26

Chapter 3: Key Settings to Activate 28

Transfer Files Instantly with Quick Share 28

Set Up and Use Music Share 30

Attend to Calls from Your Connected Devices 34

Link Your Phone to Your Computer......................... 35

Show Battery Percentage in the Status Bar 36

Get Rid of the App Tray or Customize it 37

Power and Volume Keys Shortcut 38

Get Pop-up Chat Heads for your Messaging App 39

Use Your Device to Scan Documents 40

Move the Google Search Bar to the Bottom 40

Enable Caller ID and Spam Protection 42

Enable Digital Wellbeing 43

Using Samsung Finder...45

Chapter 4: Taking Screenshots on the Galaxy S20 48

Screenshot Using a Key Combination............................ 48

Swipe Palm to Take Screenshot..................................... 49

Screenshot Using Bixby Voice.. 51

Capture More with Scroll Capture 52

Chapter 5: Maximize Battery Life of your Phone 54

Activate Night Mode 54

Switch to FHD Display 55

Disable Always on Display... 56

Adaptive Battery 59

Power Modes 63

Optimize Settings... 64

Reduce Screen Timeout 66

Enable Fast Charging...67

Wireless PowerShare 68

Chapter 6: Customize the Home Screen and Lock Screen
.... 69

Display Icons in the Lock Screen...................... 69

Discover New Sets of Clock Faces 71

Stylize the Icons 73

Add a Music Controller to Lock Screen............. 75

Display Emergency Contact on the Lock Screen 76

Lock Home Screen Layout 77

Enable Landscape Mode for Home Screens.......... 78

Quick Settings Panel..................................... 78

Accommodate More App Icons on Home screen Grid... 81

Activate Navigation Gestures 83

Explore the Overview Selection Mode 85

Show App Suggestions in Recent Apps.............. 85

Add Finder to Home Screen............................ 87

Tweak Home Screen For Notification Panel........ 89

Chapter 7: Manage Google Assistant on S20......... 91

Accessing the Google Assistant 91

Access Google Assistant without the Home Button 92

Make a Call with Google Assistant................... 93

Send a Message with Google Assistant............. 93

Search with Google Assistant 94

Get Direction with Google Assistant............................. 94

Open an App with Google Assistant 94

Disable Google Assistant... 94

Change Your Digital Assistant to Alexa 95

Chapter 8: Bixby 96

Using Bixby.. 96

Changing Bixby Settings 96

Bixby Voice 98

Bixby Marketplace 99

Using Bixby Routines 100

Bixby Vision 101

Remove Bixby From Home Screen 103

Remap Bixby Button 104

Turn off Bixby Voice wake-up and listening 106

Chapter 9: The Edge Screen..108

Using the Edge Panel 108

Brighten Up Your Notifications with Edge Lighting 109

Tweak Edge Handles 111

Chapter 10: Camera/ Video Tips 114

Shoot 8k Video on Galaxy S20 114

Edit 8K Videos...118

Remove Flickering from Your Videos 120

Add a Trippy Audio Track 121

Loop and Reverse.. 122

Extend the Timer.. 125

Customize Slow Motion Videos 126

Adjust the Motion Detection Box 129

Add a Filter to your Videos................................... 130

Enable Scene Optimizer 131

Activate Shot Suggestion...................................... 133

Live Focus Modes 135

Explore the Food Mode 137

Automatically Correct Wide-Angle Shots 140

Advanced Recording Options 142

Switch on Videos Stabilization............................... 144

Rearrange Camera Modes 146

Hide Front Camera 149

Take Photos with Palm.. 151

Chapter 11: Audio Experience................................. 153

Play with Sound Settings (Separate App Sounds) 153

Customize Sound Based on Age 154

Dolby Atmos 157

Using UHQ Upscaler.. 159

Change Bluetooth Audio Codec.......................................160

Turn Off Unnecessary Sounds 162

Chapter 12: Explore the Sound Assistant App 164

Increase Volume Step 165

Save and Share EQ Settings 166

Manage Volume for Individual Apps............................. 167

Personalize Sound Profiles... 170

Chapter 13: Device Security 172

In-Display Ultrasonic Fingerprint Scanner 172

Enable Fingerprint Icon... 173

The Alternate Look Feature 175

Activate Lockdown Mode 177

Hide Sensitive Apps... 178

How to Unhide Apps 180

Hide Albums in Gallery 180

Secured Folder 182

Hide Sensitive Files with Secured Folder 183

Find My Mobile..185

Chapter 14: Manage Your Notification Settings 187

View the Notification panel 187

Customize Your Quick Settings......................................188

Touch and Hold to See Notifications 189

Snooze alerts 191

Set Notification Reminders 193

Enable Flashlight Notifications 194

Chapter 15: Wi-fi Calling 196

Enable Wi-Fi Calling on the Galaxy S20 196

Enable Wifi Calling from the S20 Dialer 197

Using the Google Duo in the Phone Dialer 198

Chapter 16: Maximizing Display on the Galaxy S20 200

Always On Display 200

Always on Display (AOD) Themes 202

Max Out the Display Resolution 203

Screen brightness 204

Change Refresh Rate 204

Screen mode 206

Blue light filter 206

Enable One-Handed Mode 207

One-Hand Operation + App..210

Switch to Vivid Display 213

Chapter 17: Advanced Features of the S20 215

Dual Messenger 215

Get the Good Lock App 217

Assistant Menu 221

Pin Windows Feature 223
Split-screen apps 226

Introduction

Congratulations on purchasing the latest addition to the Samsung family, the S20 series. Now, you need a well-illustrated user guide that contains all the hidden tips and tricks to help you to maximize the full potentials of your Samsung S20. This user guide contains all the hidden tricks and tips that you need to know to familiarize yourself with the powerful Samsung S20, S20+, and S20 Ultra.

The Galaxy S20 series is a powerful flagship phone that comes with several new features, some of which are not yet available in any other smartphone brand in the world today. You have the advanced cameras, smooth 120Hz display, 100X zoom, and other amazing features packed in a compact design.

There is a whole lot to know about these new Samsung devices.

Let's get started.

The Layout of the Samsung S20 Series

Samsung Galaxy S20 5G

Front camera

Flash

Volume keys

Side key

Rear cameras

Fingerprint
scanner

USB charger/Audio port

Samsung Galaxy S20+ 5G

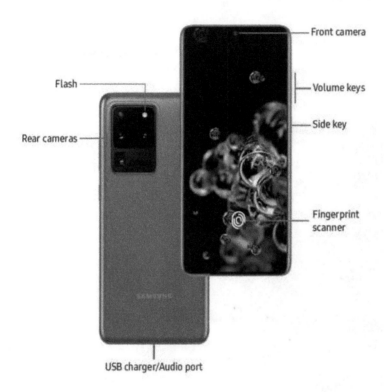

Front camera

Flash

Volume keys

Side key

Rear cameras

Fingerprint
scanner

USB charger/Audio port

Samsung Galaxy S20 ULTRA 5G

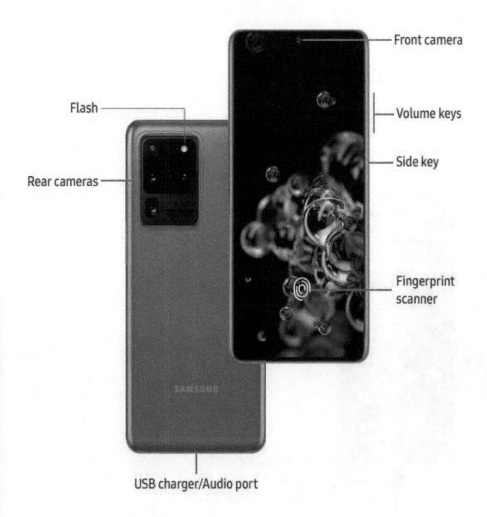

Front camera

Flash

Volume keys

Side key

Rear cameras

Fingerprint
scanner

USB charger/Audio port

Chapter 1: Getting Started/ Unboxing the Samsung S20

SIM Installation

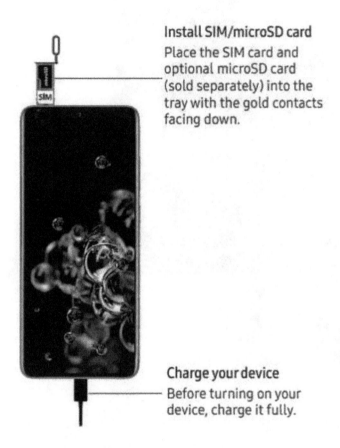

Install SIM/microSD card

Place the SIM card and optional microSD card (sold separately) into the tray with the gold contacts facing down.

Charge your device

Before turning on your device, charge it fully.

How to Set up the Samsung Galaxy S20 Series

Follow the steps below to set up your new S20 device:

- Insert your SIM card into the SIM tray before you power on your phone.

- Select your language at the "Let's go" screen, then click on the blue arrow to begin the process of setting up your new phone

- Read the terms and conditions, tick the box beside 'I **have read and agree to all of the above.**'
- Click on **Next.**

- Follow the instructions on your screen to restore your content from an old device or click on **'Skip this for Now.'**

- Click on **Next.**

- Select your Wi-fi network. You may be required to input your password. Then tap **Next.**

- Sign in to your Google account with your existing details or create a new account, then click on **Next** to proceed.

- Review Google's terms of service and click on **"I agree"** to proceed.

- To restore your previously saved backups, follow the instructions on your screen or click on **'Don't Restore.'**

- Your device will then prompt you to set up your fingerprints, facial recognition, and password or PIN. You may also skip this stage for now.

- Read through the Google services page, toggle on the options you need then click on **'Accept.'**

- Read and choose additional apps you want to download and install during the initial set up.

- Click on **OK.**

- Create your Samsung account or log in with your existing details.

- Review and agree to the presented terms and conditions, then click on **Next.**

- Restore your saved data from Samsung Cloud or click on **Skip.**

- Click **Finish** once done and begin to use your new phone.

Power On Your Device

To power on your device,

- Press and hold down on the side key until the screen lights up.

Switch Off Your Device

To turn the phone off,

- Go to the notification panel

- Click on **Power** ⏻

- Then click on **Power Off** ⏻

- Confirm your action when prompted

Here's another way to turn off your device

- Press the Volume down and side keys at the same time.

Restart Your Device

- Go to the notification panel

- Click on **Power** ⏻

- Then click on **Restart** ⟲

Auto- Restart Your Device

You can set your device to auto-restart at a specified time. Go to settings

- Tap **Device Care**

- Click on the 3-dot icon at the right top corner of your screen

- Then select **Auto Restart**

- Choose your scheduled time and date

- Enable the feature before you exit the menu.

With this option enabled, your phone will automatically restart once a week at the specified time and date. This will help your phone to run smoother and better.

Transfer Data From an Old Device

You can use Smart Switch to move videos, messages, calendars, notes, photos, contacts, and more from your old device to the S20.

To do this,

- Go to settings
- Click on **Accounts and backup**
- Then click on **Smart Switch**
- Follow the prompts on your screen and select the contents you want to move

Note: Ensure that your battery is fully charged before attempting this as it may drain your battery fast.

Double Tap to Wake Up

The display feature of the Galaxy S20 series shows you a preview of the battery percentage, notifications, as well as the time and date. You can also use face unlock or ultrasonic fingerprint scanner to wake the phone. But, the 'double-tap to wake' feature is more helpful when you need to wake your screen with just the power key. Enable this feature with the steps below:

- Go to Settings
- Click on **Advanced Features**
- Click on **Motion and Gestures**
- Now toggle on the **Double Tap to Wake Up** option.

Lift to Wake Feature

This feature, once enabled, allows you to unlock your phone just by staring into the phone. Bring the phone close to your face, and the device will scan your eyes to confirm ownership before unlocking the phone. This is particularly useful to persons that unlock their phone via biometric options like the iris sensor or intelligent scan.

- Go to Settings

- Click on **Advanced features**

- Tap **Motions and gestures**

- Then toggle on the switch for **Lift to Wake**

Force-close Apps

There are times when an app is hanging. In times like this, follow the steps below to force-close the app:

- Click on the app switcher button to display all your recently used apps

- Then swipe up on the preview of an app to force-close the app

- To close all the apps at the same time, tap the **Close All** button at the bottom of the screen

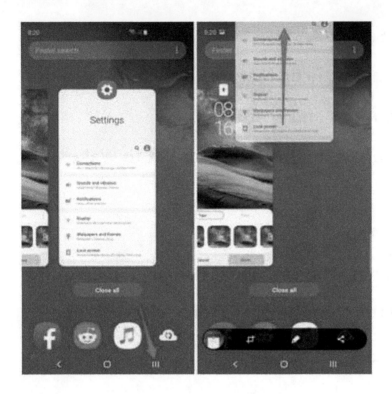

Status Icons

Battery full

Battery low

Charging

Mute

Vibrate

Airplane mode

Bluetooth active

Wi-Fi active

Location active

Alarm

Notification icons

Missed calls

Call in progress

Call on hold

New message

Voicemail

New email

Download

Upload

WI-Fi available

App update

Setup Samsung Backup

When you first set up your phone, you will receive a prompt to sign in to your Samsung account to be able to perform functions like download apps from the Galaxy store or set up the Samsung Pay. Apart from this, it also allows you to enjoy Samsung's backup service. Your device will be routinely backed up so that you can easily restore things like installed apps, or even the home screen layout of a previous Samsung device with just a few taps. Follow the steps below to check that the Samsung backup is enabled:

- Go to **Settings.** Click on **Accounts and backup**
- Tap **Samsung Cloud**

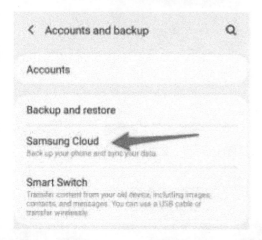

- Click on the 3-dot icon at the right top corner of your device. Click on **Settings**

- Select the first option **Sync and Auto-Backup Settings.**

- Go through the list on the next screen to confirm that all you need to back up is included in the list.

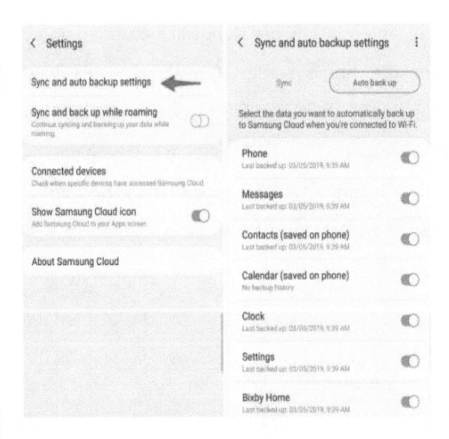

Chapter 2: Side Key Settings

Let's explore how to customize the shortcuts assigned to the S20 side key.

Double Press

To choose what happens when you press the side key twice

- Go to settings
- Click on **Advanced Features** ✿.
- Then click on **Side Key**
- Click on **Double Press** to enable the feature then choose from the displayed option:
  1. Open app 2. Open Bixby 3. Quick launch camera (default)

Press and Hold

To choose what happens when you press and hold the side key,

- Go to settings
- Click on **Advanced Features** ✿.

- Then click on **Side Key**

- Click on **Press and Hold** to enable the option, then choose from the displayed option

  1. Power off menu 2. Wake Bixby (default)

Chapter 3: Key Settings to Activate

Transfer Files Instantly with Quick Share

If you receive and share photos and files frequently, you may want to enable the **Quick Share feature.** This feature allows you to share files to other tablets and phones quickly via Wi-fi direct. Now, let's look at how to set up Quick Share

- Pull down the notification bar and long-press on the **Quick Share** icon.

- Now select who should be able to share files with you: **Everyone** or **Contacts only**

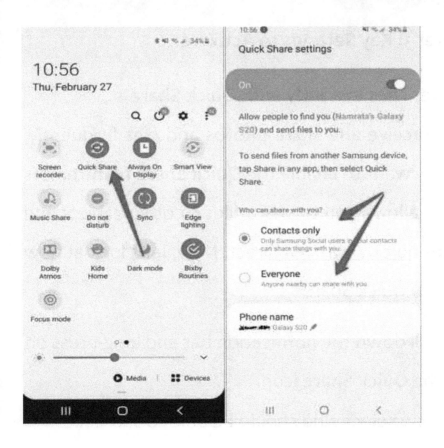

- Now, edit your phone name for easy recognition.

- Go to the sender's phone, pull down the Quick Settings bar and click on the Phone Visibility icon to activate it

- Once enabled, the compatible phones will pop up on the sharing screen

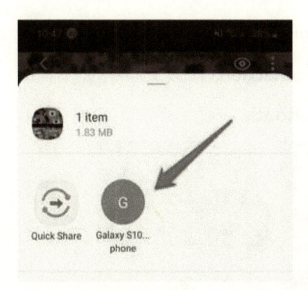

- Click on the one you want to complete the sharing in seconds.

Set Up and Use Music Share

This feature allows your friends and family members to play music from their phones via your Bluetooth speakers without connecting directly to your Bluetooth speakers. Both phones have to be connected to the same Wi-fi for this feature to work. Your S20 serves as the conduit for connecting their phones with the speakers.

To set up this feature,

- Go to Settings

- Click on **Connections**

- Select **Bluetooth**

- Then click on **Advanced**

- Now toggle on the option for **Music Share**

- Click on **Music Share** to customize sharing options

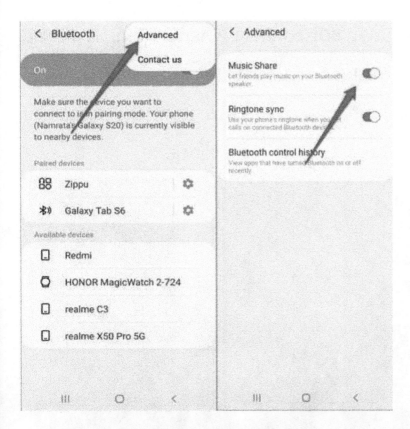

- On the next screen, set the option for **'Share devices with'** to **Contacts only** so that only persons on your contact list can access the feature

- Click on **'Ask for permission to connect'** and choose your preference from the available options: **Don't ask** or **Every time**

- The option **"Disconnect when nothing is played for"** is used to deactivate your Bluetooth devices when not in use. Choose from the displayed option as suits your preference.

- Now that you have set up the Music Share, proceed to connect your S20 to a Bluetooth speaker in your home.

- Your phone will then show on the Bluetooth speaker list of your contacts, and they can connect directly and begin playing.

Attend to Calls from Your Connected Devices

With this feature, you can connect your Samsung phones with your tablets so that if you do not have your S20 with you at any time, you can still use the tablet to receive your text and calls from the Galaxy S20. Ensure to sign in using your Samsung details on all the devices you want to connect or link. To enable this feature,

- Go to settings
- Click on **Advanced Settings**
- Toggle on the **Call & text on other devices** option
- All the connected devices will appear on the list.

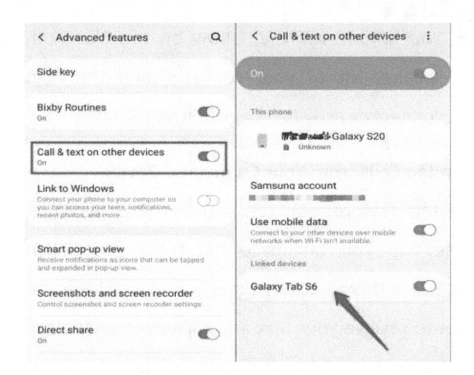

Link Your Phone to Your Computer

This action will enable you to send out messages directly from your computer or even transfer photos from your phone to your computer. But, you will need to log in using your Microsoft account on your phone and computer to be able to use this feature.

- Go to settings
- Click on **Advanced features**

- Toggle on the **Link to Windows** option, and your phone will walk you through the remaining setup.

- Easy and fast.

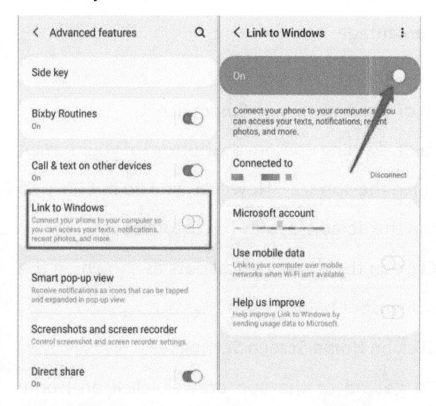

Show Battery Percentage in the Status Bar

By default, you cannot view the battery percentage on the status bar, but you can turn it on from your phone settings. To activate this option,

- Go to settings

- Click on **Notifications**

- Tap **Status Bar**

- Then toggle on the switch for **Show Battery Percentage**

Get Rid of the App Tray or Customize it

By default, swiping up from the bottom of your screen will launch the app tray. However, you do not have to maintain the default layout. To customize

- Click on the three vertical dots as shown on the screenshot below

- Click on **Home Screen Settings**

- To get rid of the app drawer, click on **Home Screen Layout**

- Then set the option to **Home Screen Only**

Power and Volume Keys Shortcut

You can quickly access the accessibility settings of your phone by using the volume and power keys. To activate this feature

- Go to settings
- Click on **Accessibility**
- Select **Advanced settings**
- Click on **Power and Volume Up keys**

- Now toggle on the feature.

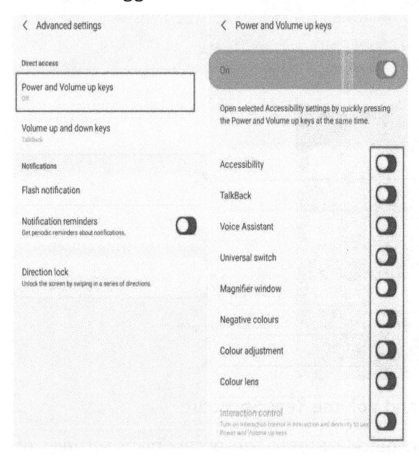

Get Pop-up Chat Heads for your Messaging App

You can set your device to display chat heads like the one used by the Facebook messenger when using any messaging app.

- Go to settings.
- Click on **Advanced features**

- Select **Smart pop-up view**

- On the next screen, you can disable or enable pop-up alerts for any app that supports the multi-window mode

Use Your Device to Scan Documents

The Samsung S20 camera can automatically reduce distortion for any documents scanned on the device, be it bank statements, receipts, letters, etc.

- Open the camera app

- Click on the cog icon to access the app settings

- Select **Scene optimizer** and switch on the option

- Also, confirm that the **Document Scan** is enabled

- Then scan a document using the rear camera of the device to see the optimizations applied.

Move the Google Search Bar to the Bottom

Do you know that you can change the position of the Google search bar? This bar is typically placed in the middle of your screen by default. To achieve this,

- Long-press on the search bar

- Then drag it to the bottom.

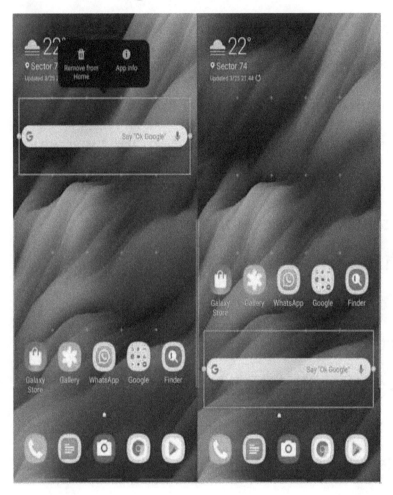

- Now, you can just click on it and begin to type your search term without fear of stretching your finger or your phone falling.

Enable Caller ID and Spam Protection

Spam calls can be a nuisance, but the good news is that the S20 has a spam protection service integrated into the dialer to prevent spam calls from getting in. To enable this feature,

- Open the dialer from your home screen
- Click on the 3-dot icon on the right
- Select **Settings**

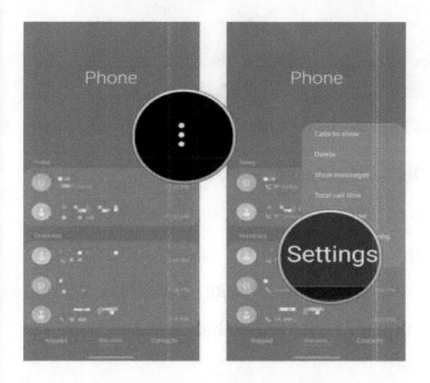

- Toggle on **Caller ID and spam protection**

- Review the privacy policy and check the boxes

- Click on **Agree** to accept and finish

Enable Digital Wellbeing

This feature helps you to monitor the amount of time you spend using your mobile device. By monitoring and tracking your phone usage, it displays a visual representation of your phone habits like the number of times you unlocked your phone, screen time, etc. To access this,

- Go to settings
- Select **Digital Wellbeing** from the displayed list.

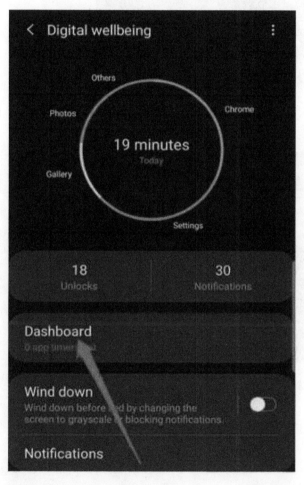

Also, you can set timers for certain apps through the Dashboard option

- Navigate to the desired app on this screen

- Click on the **'No Timer'** dropdown button

- Select your choice from the displayed list

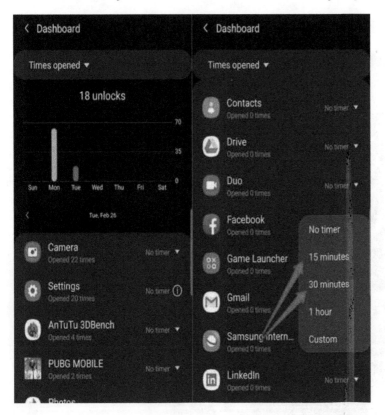

Using Samsung Finder

If you are switching from other phone brands to Samsung, you will notice that some of the options and features are hidden in obscure places. Even users who are familiar with the Samsung phones may find some of the menus confusing. Luckily, you can use the Finder app to search for anything on your device, including apps.

- Drag down the notification bar
- Click on the magnifying glass icon
- Then type your search term or keyword into the search bar. The option will display modified results as you type.

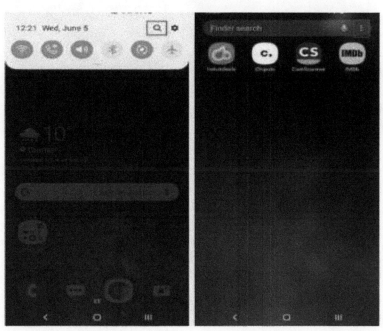

- You can edit what apps you want to exclude from the search results by clicking on the three vertical dots at the right top side of your screen

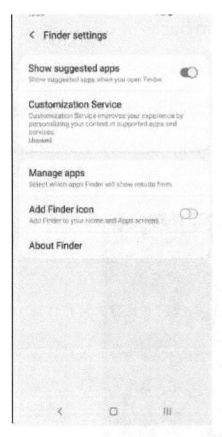

Chapter 4: Taking Screenshots on the Galaxy S20

During the day, you may have reasons to capture your screen and save or share the screenshots with others. Now, you have more than one way you can take a screenshot of your screen.

Screenshot Using a Key Combination

With the removal of the Bixby button and the power button turning into a multi-purpose button, it may seem difficult using the buttons. Find below how you can take a screenshot using the key combination

- Open the content you want to screenshot
- Now press the volume down and power button at the same time for one second. Then release both buttons
- You will see the screen flash.
- And your screenshot is ready.
- You can share the screenshot by clicking on the bottom bar that appears on your screen (far

right button), or you can view the screenshot from the notification shade.

- You can also use the center button to enter the editing mode. This mode lets you draw and crop the screenshot before saving or sharing.

Swipe Palm to Take Screenshot

This a great alternative to the usual way of taking screenshots. This feature allows you to take a screenshot by swiping the edge of your hand across your screen. To activate the feature,

- Go to settings
- Click on **Advanced features**
- Click on **Motion and Gestures**
- Now toggle on the option for **Palm Swipe to Capture**

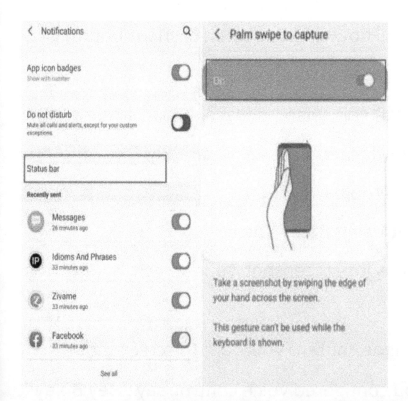

After you have enabled the swipe palm feature, now follow the steps below to capture your screen.

- Open the content you want to screenshot.

- Position your hand vertically on the right or left edge of your phone, then swipe it across the screen in one motion. Ensure to keep your hand in contact with your phone screen while doing this.

- You will now see the screen flash to confirm that the screenshot is complete.
- You can edit, share, or save the screenshot from the notification shade or directly from the on-screen toolbar.

Screenshot Using Bixby Voice

Another way to screenshot your screen is via Bixby Voice.

- Open the content you want to screenshot
- If you configured voice control, say **"Hey Bixby"** or if you have set up your phone's side button for Bixby, press and hold down the side button. A long-press of the button will automatically launch Bixby voice after you must have opened it once.
- With Bixby voice open, say, **"take a screenshot."**
- The screenshot will save in your gallery, where you can share, edit or view it.

Capture More with Scroll Capture

Regardless of the way you take the screenshot, a set of options will appear at the bottom of your screen after capturing. One of these options is called **Screen Capture.** This button is located on the left side of your screen, represented by a box that has down-facing arrows in it. This feature makes the phone to scroll through the content you have on your screen and take several screenshots. All the screenshots will then be joined together to give one complete screenshot of the whole captured content. This is particularly useful for capturing a long restaurant menu, a full webpage, or a set of multiple directions. Just click on the scroll capture button as many times as needed to capture the full content. It will automatically stop once you get to the bottom of your screen. You can also save, share, or edit the screenshots.

If you do not want to keep tapping, just hold down on the scrolling button to capture a whole page or document in one swoop.

To view the screenshot, go to your gallery app. All screenshots are saved in the screenshot album and also in the main camera roll.

Chapter 5: Maximize Battery Life of your Phone

In this chapter, we will discuss ways to make your battery last longer. Whenever you have a low battery and need the battery to take you for a little longer, endeavor to follow the steps below to save more battery life.

Activate Night Mode

One important thing you should do once you get your phone is to enable Night mode. This feature will switch your phone to dark mode and help to preserve battery life. When the phone is on night mode, the entire screen goes black, as opposed to the light mode that turns most of the pixels on which will drain your battery faster. To enable night mode

- Go to settings
- Click on **Display**
- Then toggle the switch for Night mode

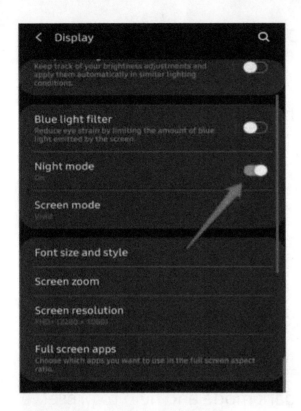

Switch to FHD Display

Your Samsung S20 allows you to switch between WQHD+ and FHD+ screen resolutions. While the former looks amazing with its sharper images and vibrant colors, the latter is best for daily usage. To switch to FHD,

- Go to settings
- Click on **Display**
- Click on Screen resolution

- Then click on FHD+ and Tap **Apply** to confirm.

- You can always switch to QHD+ whenever you want to watch a TV show or a movie

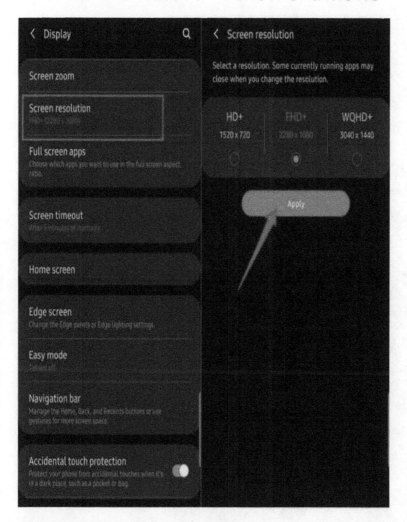

Disable Always on Display

No doubt, the Always On Display (AOD) screen looks very cool, but it also drains the battery faster. So, if you need your phone battery to last a little longer, you may switch off **Always on Display** from the Quick Settings menu.

However, the best way to use the Always-on Display option is to set it on schedule. For instance, if you do not need the Always-on Display screen during a certain period of the day, you can schedule the timing. To do this,

- Go to **Settings**

- Click on the **Lock screen**

- Click on **Always On Display**

- Tap **Display mode**

- Click on the third option and select your choice.

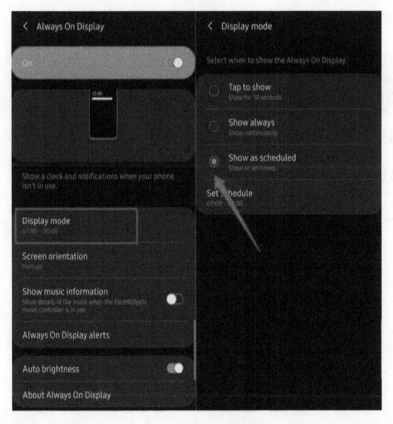

- Alternatively, click on **Tap to show.** This option will display the necessary options whenever you tap on your screen. But will return to the usual mode after ten seconds of inactivity.

Tip: when the Auto brightness setting for AOD is activated, it will automatically adjust the AOD brightness in terms of ambient brightness

Adaptive Battery

This feature, introduced in the S10 series, uses machine language to study your phone habits and app usage. With this, it can disable any app that drains the device battery unnecessarily. To enable this option,

- Go to **Settings**
- Click on **Device care**
- Click on **Battery**

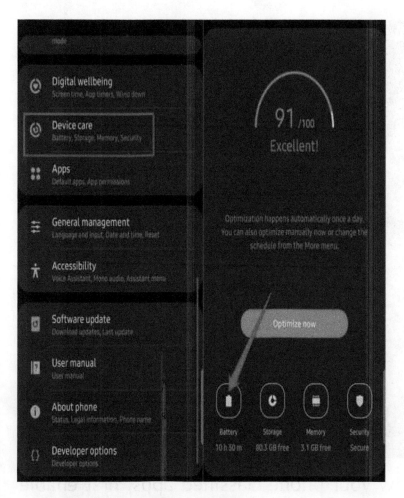

- Click on **power mode**
- Then toggle the switch beside **"Adaptive Power Saving"** to the right to enable the feature. The feature does not begin work immediately as it first needs to learn your phone habits.

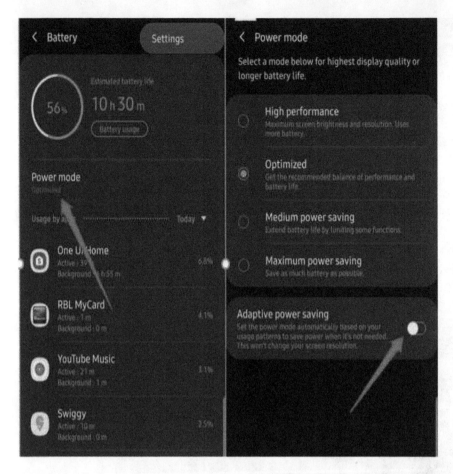

To see how your phone classified apps, first enable the Developer options. To enable developer options,

- go to Settings
- Click on **About phone**
- Tap **Software information**
- Then click on Build number 7 times.

- Once the developer option is enabled, you can now search for standby apps.

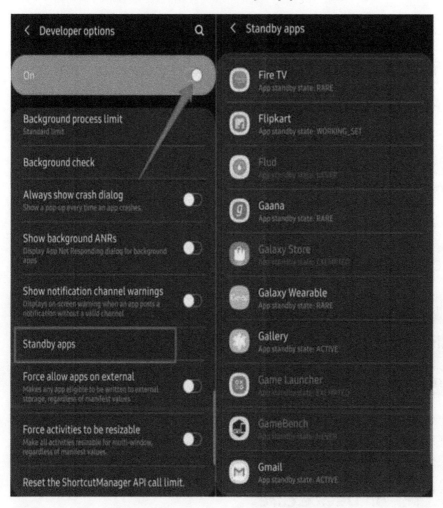

The S20 by default, categories apps into the categories below:

- Frequent
- Active

- Rare

- Working set

- Never

To manually change the categories, click on an app, and choose the option that you think is best for the app.

Power Modes

You can also check the power modes while on the battery page. The S20 series comes with three modes: Medium power-saving, high performance, and maximum power saving modes. The default setting is optimized to suit your needs, but to get the best from your battery, you may enable one of the modes.

- Go to **Settings**

- Click on **Device care**

- Tap **Battery**

- Click on **power mode**

- Then select your preferred choice

Optimize Settings

The battery optimization of the S20 series activates when you are not using your device. This feature automatically reduces screen time timeout, screen brightness, and media volume. To activate this feature,

- Go to **Settings**
- Click on **Device care**
- Tap **Battery**

- Then click on the three-dot icon at the right top side of your screen.

- Click on **Settings**

- Then search for **Optimize settings** and toggle on the switch to activate it

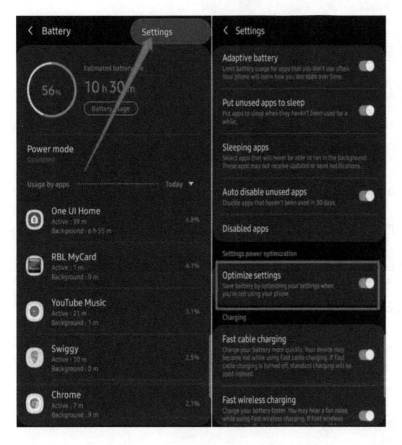

- You may also enable the options for **Adaptive Battery** and **'Put unused apps to sleep.'**

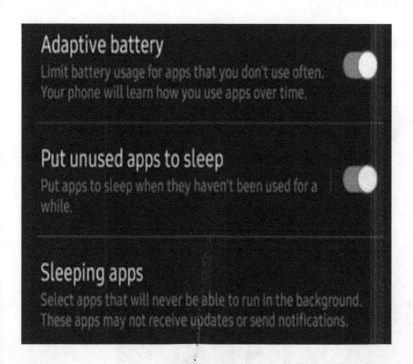

Adaptive battery

Limit battery usage for apps that you don't use often. Your phone will learn how you use apps over time.

Put unused apps to sleep

Put apps to sleep when they haven't been used for a while.

Sleeping apps

Select apps that will never be able to run in the background. These apps may not receive updates or send notifications.

Reduce Screen Timeout

Another way to save your battery is to check out the Screen timeout settings. If you are fond of dropping your phone without locking it, it will help your device battery and security if you activate screen-on time. The advisable screen-on time is 30 seconds.

To activate this change,

- Go to settings

- Click on **Display**

- Click on **Screen timeout**

- Now select your preferred time

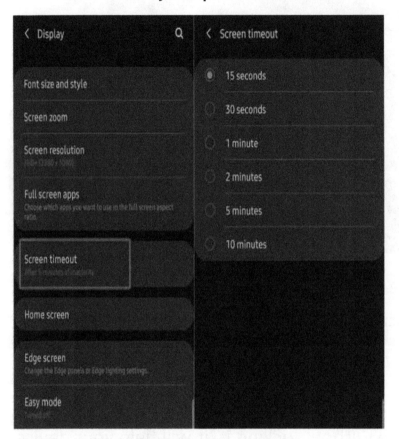

Enable Fast Charging

- Go to **Settings**

- Click on **Device care**

- Tap **Battery**

- Click on the 3-dot icon at the top right side of your screen

- Select **Settings**

- Then enable the option for fast charging, if disenabled.

Wireless PowerShare

You can use your Galaxy S20 to charge another device wirelessly. The feature responsible for this is called the Wireless PowerShare. Follow the steps below to activate this feature

- Open the quick settings panel

- Click on **Wireless PoweShare**

- Then place both phones close to each other to begin charging

Note: Ensure that your S20 has over 30% battery life remaining before you use this feature.

Chapter 6: Customize the Home Screen and Lock Screen

The Home screen and lock screen are two screens we use the most on our phones. Thanks to the Android customization options, we can now customize these screens to suit our purposes. So here are tips for the S20 home screen and lock screen.

Display Icons in the Lock Screen

Would you want your device to display all your notifications on your lock screen? Maybe not. Thankfully, the S20 has the option for you to hide your notifications. You can customize it to display only the notification icons or a brief message, just like you have on the AOD screen. This way, you get to know what the notification is about while hiding the full content. Follow the steps below to make these changes:

- Go to settings

- Click on **Lock Screen**

- Select **Notifications**

- Then click on **View Style**

- Select **Icons Only**

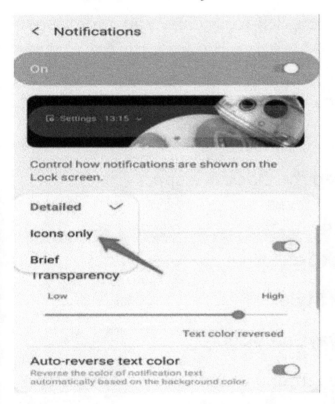

But, if you really want to see all your notifications on the lock screen, you can set the notification box to be transparent by dragging the **Transparency** bar to the right.

Discover New Sets of Clock Faces

Using the current clock faces of the Samsung devices can get boring. Thankfully, Samsung's ClockFace app has lots of stylish clock faces. Plus, you can choose your preferred color. Sadly, this is not available globally, but you can get the APK file from APK Mirror, download the file and enjoy the feature. After you must have installed the Clockface app,

- Go to settings
- Click on **Lock Screen**
- Select **Clock Style**
- Click on **Always-on Display**
- Scroll to the left end of your screen and click on the clock icon to display all the new clock faces.

- Click on it once, then tap **Apply.**

- Now go to the **Color** tab, select your preferred color, and click the **Done** button.

- Your new AOD screen is ready.

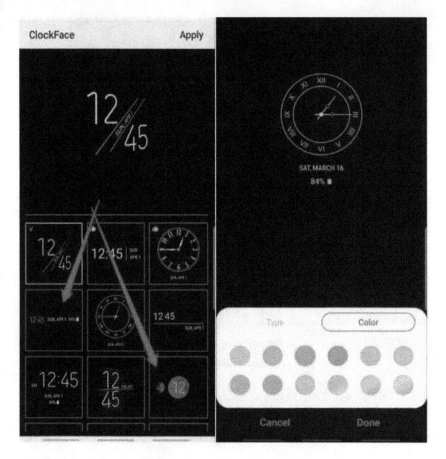

Stylize the Icons

You are not limited to using only the icon packs from Samsung as you can download several icon packs from Google play store, But you will need to use a third-party launcher like Nova Primes to use these icon packs. The icon packs that I like are the Pixel Pie icon pack and the Voxel icon pack. Do check them out.

But if you prefer the ones from One UI, you can download the icon packs on the Samsung store. To view more packs,

- Long-press on the home screen

- Click on **Themes**

- Select **Icons**

- Then click on **Top**

- Click on your preferred one, download, and click the **Apply** button.

Add a Music Controller to Lock Screen

For music lovers like me, another feature you should have on your lock screen is the music controller. You do not need any third-party app to enjoy this feature. With the music controller enabled, whenever you launch music streaming apps, you will see the controls displayed on the lock screen, and you can also access the app without waking or unlocking your phone.

To enable this feature,

- Go to the settings app
- Click on **Lock Screen**
- Select **Face Widgets**
- Then toggle on the **Music** switch

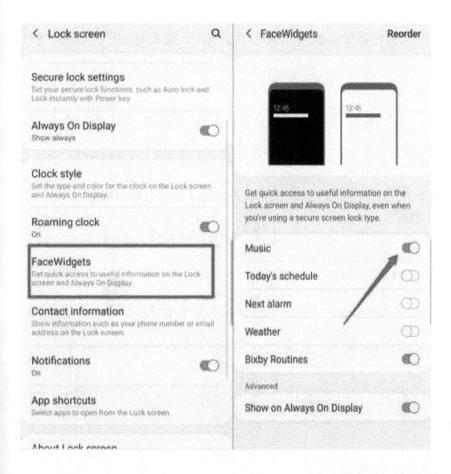

Display Emergency Contact on the Lock Screen

It is only wise to display an emergency contact number on the screen of your device. To do this,

- Go to settings
- Click on **Lock Screen**

- Click on **Contact Information,** set your preferred emergency contact

- The contact details will now show on your lock screen. However, if it doesn't, restart your phone. Double-click on the lock screen to display your wallpaper and the contact.

Lock Home Screen Layout

At times, we move the home screen layout in error. Now you can prevent the home icons from being moved by enabling the Lock Home Screen layout. To do this

- Go to settings

- Click on **Display**

- Select **Home Screen**

- Now toggle on the switch for **Lock Home Screen Layout**

- With this setting in place, you will be unable to move icons within the home screen.

Enable Landscape Mode for Home Screens

While most apps on your S20 can switch between the landscape and portrait modes, the home screen remains in portrait mode by default, regardless of how you hold the phone. The steps below will guide you on how to enable landscape mode

- Go to the home screen and long-press on any blank part of the screen
- Click on **Home Screen Settings**
- Navigate to **Portrait mode only** and move the switch to the left to disable the option
- Now your home screen can also rotate like other apps

Quick Settings Panel

The Quick Settings Panel on your device contains shortcuts for device functionality and settings, but you will need to re-arrange the shortcuts for faster access as well as increase the grid size of the shortcuts. To do this,

- Swipe down from the top of your phone's display until the Quick Settings Panel covers your screen

- Click on the three-dot menu at the top right side of your screen

- Then click on **Button Grid**

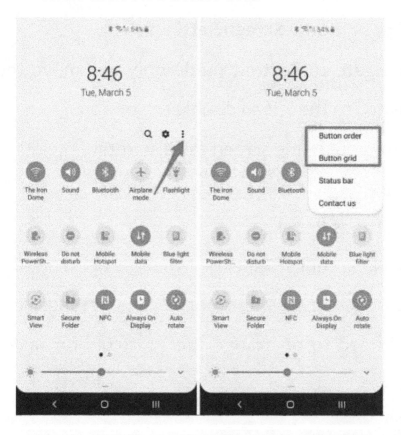

- You will see some options displayed at the bottom of the screen. Choose the grid that suits your preference. The 5x3 option can accommodate almost all settings on one pane.
- Now rearrange the icons to your preference using the **Button Order** option from the same view.
- The first six shortcuts you choose will be visible whenever you access the notification pane
- Tap **Done** once satisfied.

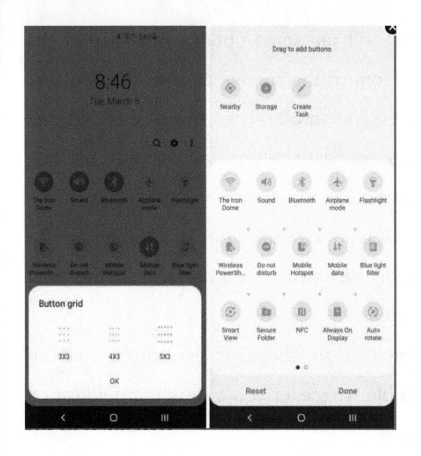

Accommodate More App Icons on Home screen Grid

You can adjust the home screen app grid to accommodate more app icons on the screen of your device.

- Return to the home screen and long-press on any blank area there

- Then click on **Home Screen Settings** at the bottom of your screen

- Click on **Home Screen Grid** and modify the grid size to suit your preference.
- To adjust the app screen grid, follow the steps above to access the **Home Screen Settings,** then

click on **'App Screen Grid'** and adjust to your preference.

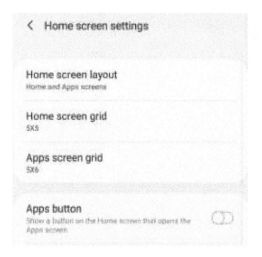

Activate Navigation Gestures

If you are yet to join the gestures party, follow the steps below

- Open the Settings app
- Click on **Display**
- Select **Navigation bar**
- Then click on **Full-Screen Gestures** to activate
- You can also click on **button buttons** to change the button order.

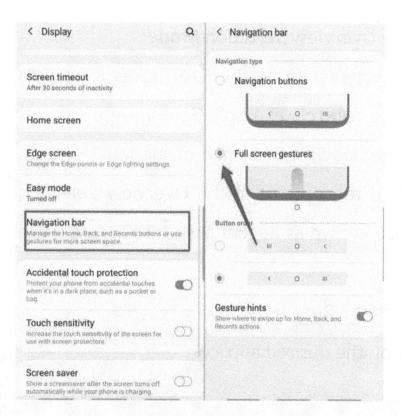

- After this is enabled, you can always swipe up from the left side of your screen to pull up the Overview selection.

- Swipe up from the bottom right side of your screen to go back.

- To go to the home screen, swipe up from the middle of the screen

Explore the Overview Selection Mode

The operating system of the S20 makes it easy to access some controls like Split Screen, App Info, or Pop up view. Now, rather than diving into settings, you can find the options in the Overview Selection section, also known as Recent Menu. To access these controls,

- Launch the Recent menu
- Click on the desired app icon

Show App Suggestions in Recent Apps

Another feature of the One UI is the 'Recent Apps Suggestion,' which is different from the apps' suggestion in the app drawer. This particular feature shows you all the apps you used recently. To use this feature, simply pull up the Recents menu, also known as the **Overview section,** and you will see all your frequently used apps at the bottom of your screen. Of course, you need to enable this feature before you can use it. To activate,

- Launch the Recents menu
- Click on the 3-dot button at the right top side of your screen
- Click on **Settings**
- Then enable the option for **Suggested Apps**

Add Finder to Home Screen

Most Samsung users will agree that the Finder is one of the best features of this operating system. This feature allows you to search for calendar events, settings, and apps. The good news is that you can customize the Finder settings as you like. But one of its most useful settings is the shortcut settings. To add the Finder Shortcut to your home screen,

- Open the app drawer
- Click on the 3-dot menu in the search button
- Then click on **Finder settings**
- Click on **Add Finder**

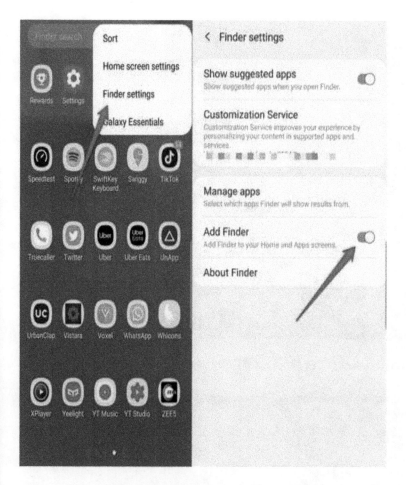

- On the next screen, drag the 1 x 1 icon to the home screen (see screenshot)

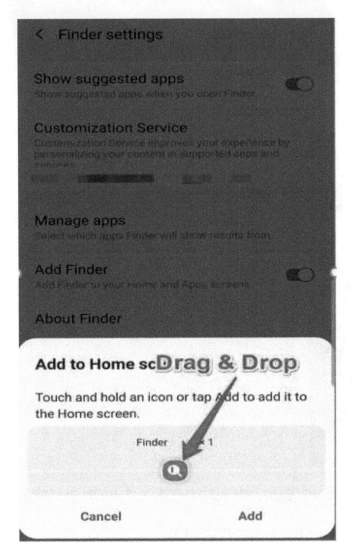

So when next you need to search, just click on the Finder icon.

Tweak Home Screen For Notification Panel

Do you find it difficult to reach the notification panel? It will be so much easier if a download swipe on your home screen can display all the notifications, and yes, there is a way to enable this. To enable this setting,

- Long-press on a blank space on the home screen
- Then click on **Home Screen Settings**
- On the next page, navigate to **Quick-open notification panel** and toggle on the switch

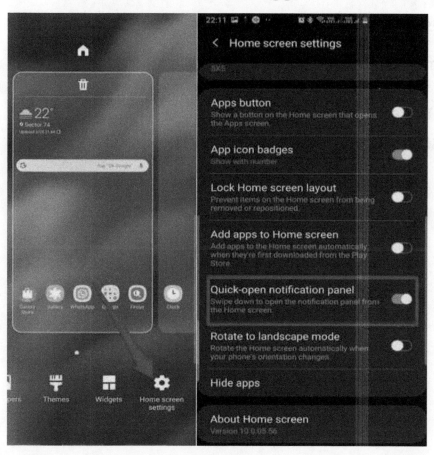

Chapter 7: Manage Google Assistant on S20

On the one hand, you have Bixby as Samsung's digital assistant, on the other hand, you have the Google assistant for android phones. You can also install Alexa to give you a third option.

Accessing the Google Assistant

This feature is in sync with your Google account, so it works with anything you previously set-up Google Assistant to do. To access this virtual assistant,

- Long-press on the on-screen home button to launch the Google assistant
- Now speak to Google to get your search results

Access Google Assistant without the Home Button

For those who set up their device to use gestures instead of the navigation bar,

- Swipe and hold from the bottom middle of the screen, the part where the home button should be.

- You will then see the Google Assistant pop-up

Alternatively, you can enable OK Google to activate Voice for the Google Assistant. To do this,

- Launch the Google app

- Click on the 3-dot icon on the top left

- Click on **Settings**

- Select **Voice**

- Then click on **"Ok Google" Detection**

- Toggle on the options for '**From Any Screen**' and '**From Google Search App**'

- Return to the Voice screen and ensure that your Language is set to English (US).And you are done

Make a Call with Google Assistant

- Launch the Google Assistant and say "Call," followed by the receiver's name or the number you wish to call.

- The assistant will then dial the number

Send a Message with Google Assistant

- Launch the Google Assistant and say "Message," followed by the saved contact's name or the number you wish to send the message to as well as the content of the message. Then say **Send**

Search with Google Assistant

- Launch the Google Assistant and say your search terms. You will see your results displayed on the screen.

Get Direction with Google Assistant

- Launch the Google Assistant and say "Directions To," followed by the location or address.
- The direction will pop-up on the map

Open an App with Google Assistant

- Launch the Google Assistant and say "Open," followed by the name of the app

Disable Google Assistant

To remove the Google assistant from the home button shortcut, follow the steps below

- Go to settings. Click on **Apps**
- Click on the 3-dot icon at the top right of your screen. Select **Default apps**
- Now click on **Device Assistance App**

- Then click on **Device Assistance App** again and set the option to **None.**

- So when next you long-press on the home button, nothing will happen

Change Your Digital Assistant to Alexa

You can choose to use Alexa as your digital assistant rather than the Google Assistant. First, install the Alexa app, then follow the steps below to set it up as your default virtual assistant:

- Go to settings. Click on **Apps**

- Click on the 3-dot icon at the top right side of your screen

- Select **Default apps**

- Now click on **Device Assistance App**

- Then click on **Device Assistance App** again and choose **Alexa.**

Chapter 8: Bixby

Bixby is Samsung's virtual assistant, different from the Google Assistant, Siri, and Alexa. Samsung designed the virtual assistant to attempt to anticipate what your needs are and send you contextualized reminders. Bixby can send messages, edit photos, compose emails, remind you of important dates, all on command. The virtual assistant also controls some smart home devices like your TVs, smart fridges, and several Samsung devices. We will look at everything you need to know about Bixby

Using Bixby

It is straightforward to pull up Bixby and Bixby Voice. To do this, simply press and hold your power button and the virtual assistant will pop-up.

Changing Bixby Settings

The S20 series comes loaded with the three versions of the virtual assistant: Bixby Vision, Bixby Home, and

Bixby Voice. Here, we will talk about where to find each setting.

To access Bixby Home,

- Swipe right across your home screen.

To access the settings for your interactive cards,

- Click the 3-dot icon in the top right
- Then click on **Cards**
- Now add the cards you want to see or remove the ones you do not want to see.

To change the email address linked to your Bixby Home,

- Click the 3-dot icon in the top right
- Then click on **Settings**
- On the next screen, change the email address. You can also change the content providers mapped to your Bixby Home on this screen. (This option allows you to send your location data to

specific apps to give helpful and customized data. This is currently limited to Fourspace and Uber)

Bixby Voice

This part of Bixby houses most of the settings. To access it,

- long-press your power button.
- Now click on the 3-dot icon to discover further options like **Quick Commands, Tutorials, and Settings.**
- Click on **Settings** to modify everything from whether Bixby should respond when your phone is locked to your Voice Style.
- Click on **Quick Command** to tie phrases and actions together. For instance, you can customize the virtual assistant to set the alarm and put off all lights when you say, " I am going to bed."

But first, you need to install the software and complete the Bixby's Voice tutorial before you can invoke the voice assistant. You can activate Bixby Voice by saying "Hey Bixby" or pressing down the Bixby button while you talk.

You can also customize Bixby Voice like changing the gender of the assistant, shortening lengthy commands to a single phrase or word, etc.

Bixby Marketplace

This feature is a new addition to Bixby. It allows you to customize your Bixby experience further. You can easily add new services, referred to as 'capsules,' as well as check what you can do with the existing capsules. To go to the marketplace,

- Open Bixby
- Then swipe left to go to the Bixby Marketplace

- When you get into the marketplace, you can browse through the available categories or search for specific capsules.

Using Bixby Routines

This feature was introduced in Galaxy S10 Plus, wherein the digital assistant studies your behavior and offers ways you can save more time. The suggestions can range from launching apps that meet specific requirements to tweaking system settings. Also, you can add your customized routines. With this feature, you can program your phone to behave in a defined manner. So, you can set your device to default to silent mode when the clock strikes 9 PM.

To explore this feature,

- Go to Settings
- Click on **Advanced Features**
- Then tap on **Bixby Routines**

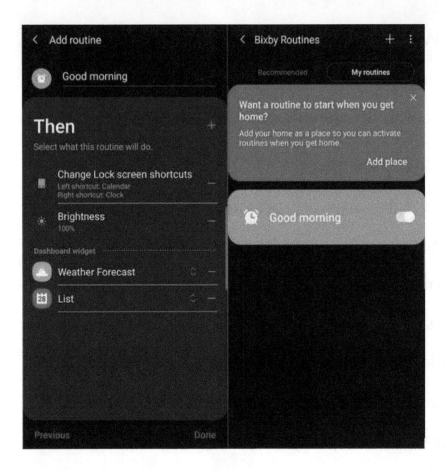

Bixby Vision

Samsung integrated Bixby with your Internet, camera, and gallery apps to present you with a deeper understanding of the things you see.

Camera

Bixby vision is present on the camera viewfinder to help with a better understanding of what you see.

- Open the camera app

- Click on **More**

- Tap **Bixby Vision** 👁

- Then follow the prompts on your screen

Gallery

Bixby Vision can also be used on images and pictures stored in the gallery app

- Open the gallery app. Click on a picture to open

- Click on **Bixby Vision** 👁

- Then follow the prompts on your screen

Internet

You can use Bixby Vision to find out more about an image in the internet app.

- Go to the internet

- Click and hold an image until a pop-up shows on your screen

- Click on **Bixby Vision** 👁

- Then follow the prompts on your screen

Remove Bixby From Home Screen

If you are among the group that finds the virtual assistant intrusive, the first step you should take would be to remove the Bixby Home from your home screen. To do this,

- Long press on the home screen
- Then swipe to the right until you get to a preview of Bixby Home
- Toggle off the switch beside **Bixby Home**.

Remap Bixby Button

You can configure the Bixby button on your device to launch other apps outside Bixby.

- Double-press the Bixby button to launch Bixby
- Click on the 3-dot menu icon
- Tap **Settings**
- Then click on **Bixby key**

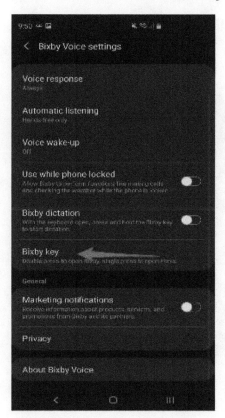

Now, you can set the Bixby key to perform two functions. You can set up the double press or single press option to activate Samsung's personal assistant while you use the remaining settings to open any other app of your choice.

For instance, if you set Bixby to open whenever you single-press the Bixby key, you can set the double-press option to open Instagram, Twitter, or any other app of your choice.

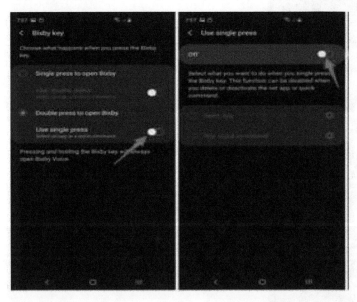

If you do not want to use the key to launch any app, you can use it to trigger a Bixby Quick Command.

Quick Command houses various device actions like reading your calendar, enabling always-on-display, and disabling DND. While these options are prebuilt into Bixby, you can go ahead to create your own commands.

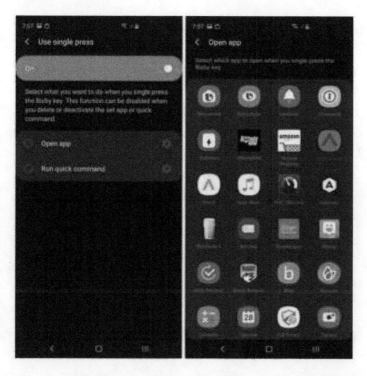

Turn off Bixby Voice wake-up and listening

If you do not want Bixby to wake up your device or you want to prevent Bixby from listening to you, you can turn the options off, only if you previously set up Bixby.

- Open Bixby
- Click on the menu button at the top right side of your screen
- Select **Settings**
- On this screen, you will find the option for **Voice Wake-up** and **Automatic Listening.** Turn off both options to disable them.

Chapter 9: The Edge Screen

Using the Edge Panel

The Edge panel contains selected apps that you can access by swiping from the right-hand edge of your screen. Although the edge panel has some apps by default, you can modify the settings to include your favorite apps, and you can also change how this feature works.

- Go to the settings app
- Click on **Display**
- Tap **Edge screen**
- Then click on **Edge panels**
- On the next screen, you can choose to disable the feature completely, use clipboard or weather information only or select the apps or contacts that you want to show up in this view

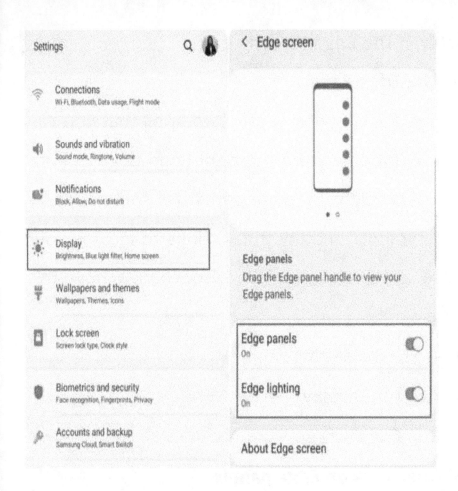

Brighten Up Your Notifications with Edge Lighting

Another exciting way to use your device's screen edges is to have them light up whenever a notification arrives. The light will replace the usual pop-up alerts and works well even when your phone is face down. To enable this feature,

- Go to the settings app

- Click on **Display**

- Tap **Edge screen**

- Then click on **Edge lighting**

- In this screen, you can disable or enable the feature, selectively activate edge lights for specific apps, choose your preferred lighting light, and lots more.

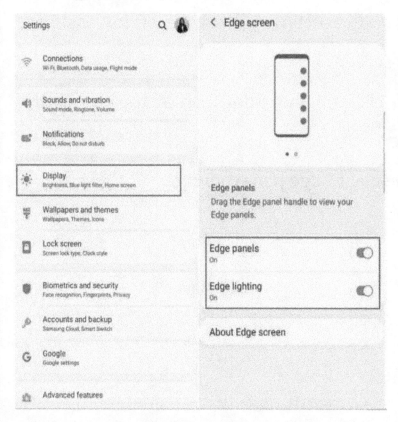

Tweak Edge Handles

One way you can handle your phone with one hand is to organize the Edge screen's handles to suit your convenience. This handle is usually located at the right edge of the Samsung screen by default, but you can always customize to suit your convenience.

- Pull out the Edge screen
- Click on the settings icon at the left lower side of your screen
- Then click on the 3-dot icon at the top of the screen
- Now select **Edge panel handle**

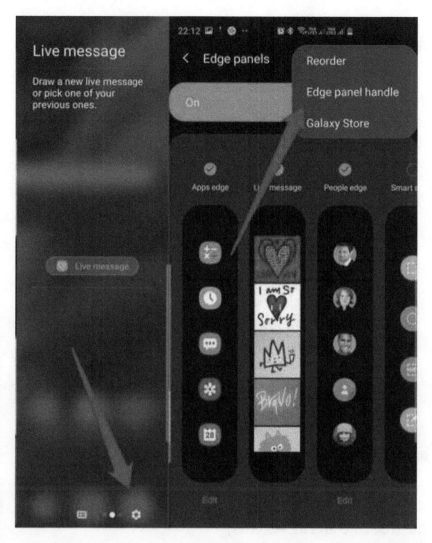

- On the next screen, you can change the side, transparency, size, and position of the handle

You may also reorder the panels to suit your convenience. To achieve this,

- Return to the previous page
- Click on the 3-dot icon again
- Then select **Reorder**

Chapter 10: Camera/ Video Tips

The camera of the S20 comes loaded with hidden settings and features which we will explore in this chapter.

Shoot 8k Video on Galaxy S20

The Samsung Galaxy S20 series is the first phone equipped with shooting 8k video, thanks to the Snapdragon 865 chipset and the all-new camera sensors. Now you can shoot videos that have 4 times the amount of pixels of the 4K. One interesting note about 8K video recording is that you can pull 33MP stills directly from the video. There is no limit to how much you can shoot, so long as you have enough storage on your phone.

Some important things to note about shooting in 8K: You can only shoot in a 16:9 format, and the frame rate is stuck at 24 frames per second while shooting at 4K gives you 60 frames per second. Also, video stabilization does not work when shooting on 4K, so if you need stable footage, it is best to use a tripod. Thirdly, not so many devices can playback 8K videos currently. Finally, a minute of 8K video uses up 800MB storage, so shooting a 5-minute 8K video will take up 4GB, which may be a lot if you do not have enough space on your device. Notwithstanding, the 8K video is still exciting, and you should try it on your new S20. Let us begin with how to shoot 8k video on your new device:

- Open the camera app
- Switch to video mode

- Click on the **Video Ratio button** to switch to 8K view

- Click on **9:16 8K** to activate 8K video recording

- You can now click the **Record** button on the viewfinder to begin shooting your 8K video

Edit 8K Videos

The default video editor of the S20 allows you to easily edit 8K footage shot on your phone, straight from the camera interface.

- Open the camera app and select the video from the media preview on the left side
- Click on the **Edit button**

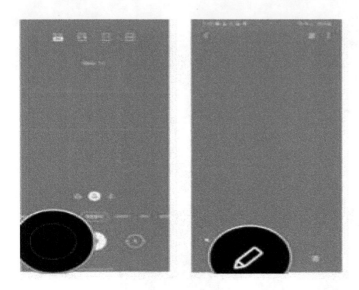

- Click on **Allow** to grant the Video editor access to your device's storage

- Now proceed to make the necessary editing from the editor's interface. You can choose to include emoji, effects and filters, trim video length, and add text. Note that when you add emoji effects or text to your video, it will convert the video to 4K.

Remove Flickering from Your Videos

To best enjoy slow-motion videos, you need light. The more light you have, the better the quality of your videos. The best time to shoot super slow-motion videos is in the mornings and middays. The video will not only be noise-less but will also eliminate unwanted shadows. But if you notice that your video has slight flickering, you can use a built-in option to remove the flickering.

- Open the video in your phone gallery

- Click on the Play slow-motion video bubble

- Click on the three-dot button at the top right side of your screen

- Then toggle the switch for **Remove flickering**

Add a Trippy Audio Track

Your Samsung S20 allows you to add a trippy song to a video to lift the mood of the video, and this feature comes with several audio tracks. To add a song

- Click on the Music bubble above the seek bar

- If accessing this module for the first time, tap **OK** on the confirmation box

- Then choose from the available songs

- All the songs in this module are arranged according to categories, making it easy for you to select and download desired songs. Ensure you have good internet coverage as you need to download most tracks before you can successfully use them.

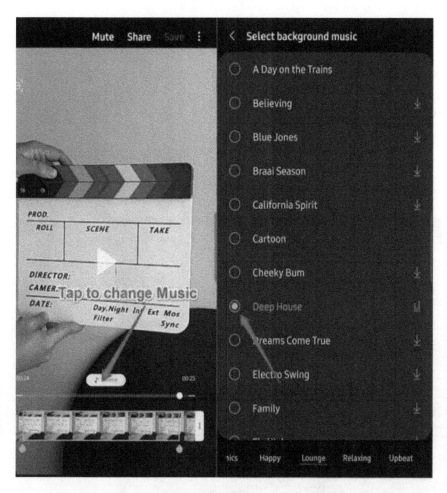

- After downloading, make the other modifications/ adjustments. Then save it

Loop and Reverse

Your Samsung S20 not only allows you to reverse a super slow-mo clip, but you can also repeat a clip in a loop. To do this

- Click on the video to launch it

- Then hit the three-dot icon

- Click on **Details**

- Three clips will display at the bottom of your screen

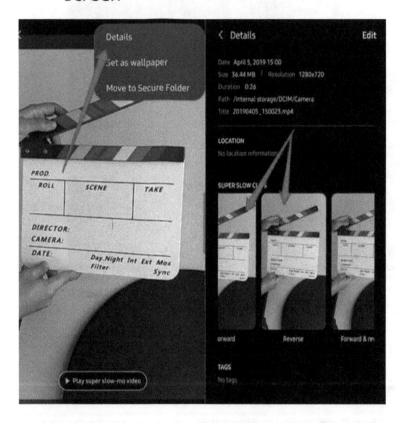

- Click on the one you like and Save as **MP4.**

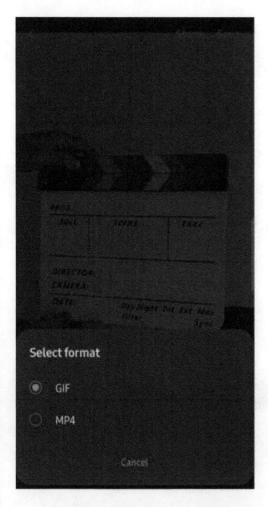

- You can now perform regular modifications like trimming or adding songs

Tip: click on the camera icon on the right side of your screen to capture a still frame from a video

Extend the Timer

The Galaxy S20 allows you to record super slow-mo videos for either 0.8 seconds or 0.4 seconds. Recording on a 0.4 seconds option gives the best results while that of 0.8 seconds maintains standard quality. 0.8 seconds of video captured at 480 fps will yield 24 seconds of playback while 0.4 seconds of video at 960 fps will produce 12 seconds of playback time.

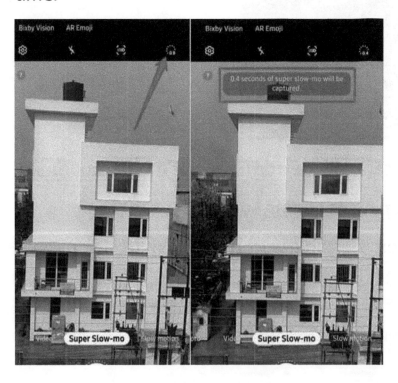

However, if you prefer the standard quality slow-mos,

- Launch the camera app

- Swipe till you get to the Super slow-motion tab

- Then click once on the timer icon at the top of your screen

Customize Slow Motion Videos

Just like the S10, the S20 has two time-frames for capturing slow-motion videos: 0.8 and 0.4 seconds. Simply click on the timer at the right upper side of your screen and select your preferred option. You also need to ensure that the Auto Detect mode is active. As the name implies, this feature ensures that recording begins immediately it detects any action.

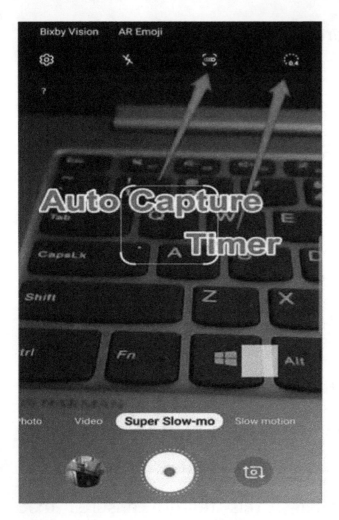

Also, check other additional settings for the super slow-motion videos. To do this

- Launch the video in the gallery app
- Click on the **Play Super slow-mo video** icon towards the bottom of the screen to launch the video in edit mode

- Now customize as you desire.

- To change the audio track, click on the little music icon and choose **Theme Music**

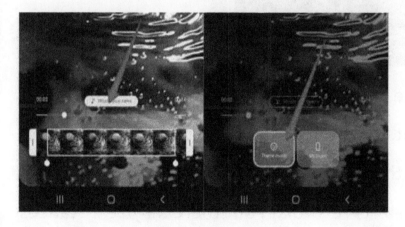

- Now the best for the last. Click on the 3-dot menu and select **Details**

- Navigate to Super slow clips

- choose any of the options to add a whimsical touch to the video: **Reverse, Forward, Loop**

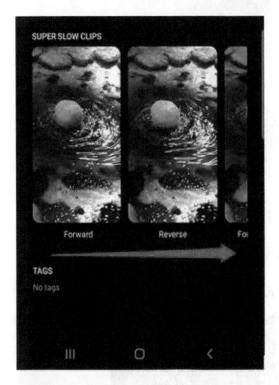

Adjust the Motion Detection Box

By default, when the camera is in the manual mode, it waits for the action to begin within the detection box before it starts recording. But there may be instances where the action happens so fast that the camera is unable to detect on time, thereby missing some critical part in the recording. To handle situations like this, simply increase the size of the focus by dragging the edges of the box.

Add a Filter to your Videos

Unfortunately, the editing suite of the Samsung S20 does not have options for filters. But you can use

third-party apps like **Inshot** to edit and share your videos with family and friends. If you want to filter and upload videos on Instagram, you can make use of the in-app filters.

Enable Scene Optimizer

The scene optimizer of the S20 series can differentiate between pets and buildings, optimize images accordingly, among many other things. To enable this feature,

- Launch the camera app
- Go to the settings by clicking on the cog-shaped icon. Then toggle on the switch for **Scene optimizer**

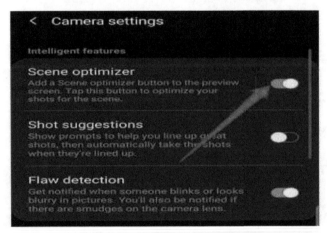

- With this feature enabled, a powder blue icon will appear each time you launch the camera app.
- To disable the feature, just click on the blue icon.

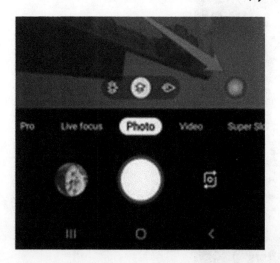

That's not all. Apart from recognizing scenes, the scene optimizer also performs other functions like Starburst and Document scan. To activate,

- Click on **Scene optimizer**
- Then toggle the switch for both the Starburst and Document scan

- Starburst converts burst of light on low-light photos to artistic effects while the Document scan, like the name implies, scans documents.

Activate Shot Suggestion

This is another exciting feature of the S20 camera. The camera uses the AI prowess of the device to detect scenarios and offer you suggestions on ways to get better shots.

Once enabled, you will see two guiding orbs on your screen (one for improving composition and the other for straightening). All you now have to do is align the focus with the orbs and take your shot.

The camera app may take a few seconds to analyze the shot. To enable the shot suggestion feature,

- Launch the camera app
- Go to the settings by clicking on the cog-shaped icon

- Then toggle on the switch for **Shot suggestions**

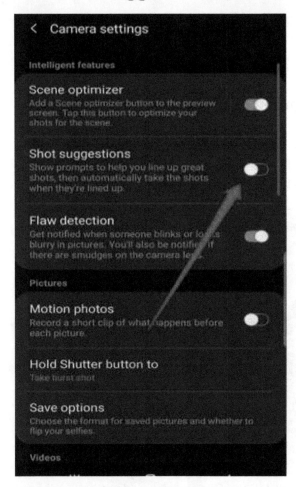

Live Focus Modes

This camera mode, introduced in the Galaxy Note 8, has four shooting modes. You can now experiment with artistic effects like the Google photos-like color pop, spiral, or Edge Blur mode. The Google color pop mode maintains the subject's colors and paints the background in white and black.

You can also reduce the blur levels by dragging the slider to the left. You can still switch to the standard blur effect if not pleased with the outcome. To do this,

- Go to your gallery and open the image
- Click on the change background effect bubble

- Select the new mode

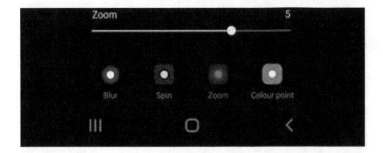

- Then click on **Apply**

This also applies to the front camera; the only exception is the frame. The frames of the front camera are a bit wide, mainly due to the use of the main camera for taking portrait shots rather than the telephoto lens.

Explore the Food Mode

This mode is an interesting one for foodies as it will not only capture the very minute details of the subject but will also give the image a rich tone. You can also use this mode to capture other colorful items to bring out their full glory. You have two ways to achieve this; either you keep the whole image in focus, or you highlight a specific area. I always prefer the first option.

Another exciting feature is the Pallete, which you can use to adjust the color and temperature of your image. Simply drag the slider until you get the best of the image.

Both the Pallete and the Radial blur are available on the tools ribbon at the top of your screen.

Automatically Correct Wide-Angle Shots

Owing to the ultra-wide mode of the S20, you can capture some fantastic wide-angle sots. The device also has a dedicated wide-angle shot correction feature that eliminates lens distortion from the edges.

Distorted window frame

The distortion is automatically removed as soon as the picture is saved.

To activate this option,

- Launch the camera app
- Go to settings by clicking on the cog-shaped icon
- Click on **Save options**
- Enable the option for **Ultra-Wide Shape Correction**
- On this same screen, enable the **RAW copies** and **HEIF pictures** option.
- The RAW copies provide a picture (when taken in Pro mode) in RAW image and JPEG formats while the latter helps to save space.

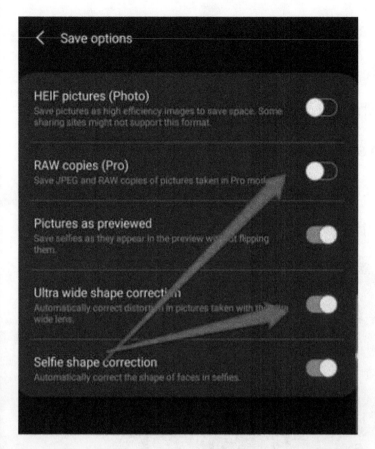

RAW photos record more information than the typical standard JPEG images, thereby making them easy to edit.

Advanced Recording Options

The HDR10+, a high dynamic range format, was first introduced in the Samsung S10. This feature optimizes the contrast and color of videos to make them look more life-like. To enable this feature,

- launch the camera app
- Click on settings
- Then click on **Advanced Recording options**
- Enable the option for **HDR10+ Video**

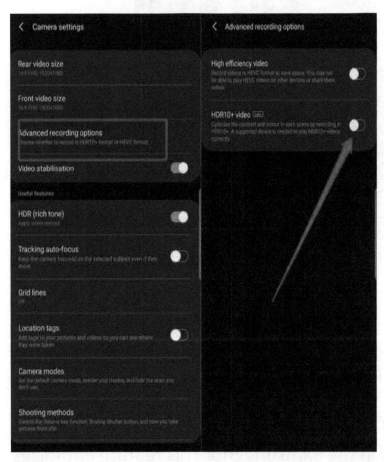

Switch on Videos Stabilization

The standard telephoto lens and wide camera are optically stabilized lenses, and so, we expect videos should be steady. But, you can take it a step further by activating video stabilization to give you smoother footages. This feature will ensure that your videos are free from wobbles and shakes.

To activate,

- Launch the camera app
- Click on settings
- Then enable the option for **Video Stabilization**

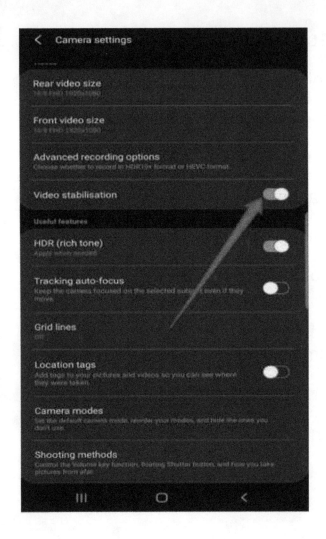

Another great stabilization feature is the **"Super Steady stabilization mode."** Represented by a hand icon in the video mode, the feature helps to capture smooth footages. However, videos under this feature are recorded in 1080p resolution.

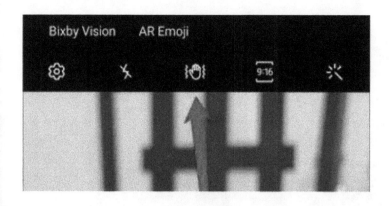

Rearrange Camera Modes

You can arrange your camera mode to have your favorites modes beside each other, like having the auto mode next to the food mode. To do this,

- Open the camera app
- Swipe right until you get to the **More** subsection
- Click on the **Edit icon** at the right lower side of your screen

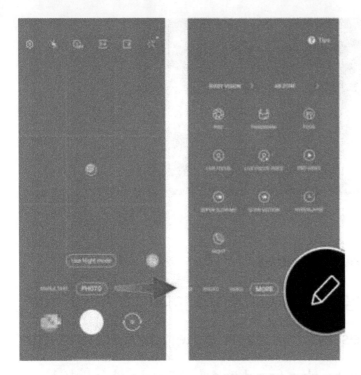

- Pull the desired shooting mode from the sub-menu onto the ribbon.

- The shooting mode should now appear in the ribbon interface, at the bottom of your screen

- Click on **Save** once you are done dragging all the desired camera modes to the ribbon

Here's another way to rearrange the camera mode.

- Launch the camera app

- Click on settings

- Click on **Camera modes**

- Click on **Edit modes**

- Rearrange the modes by dragging each one to the desired position

- Untick the modes you do not use to deactivate them and declutter your camera interface.

Also, if you want your S20 camera to launch to the last mode you used, enable this feature under the camera modes.

- Click on **Camera modes**
- Then enable the option for **Keep Using Last Mode**

Hide Front Camera

The S20 has its punch-hole camera in the top middle side of the screen, and it may become a bother when watching movies on the device. The good news is that you can hide the front camera. To do this

- Go to settings
- Click on **Display**
- Select **Full-Screen Apps**

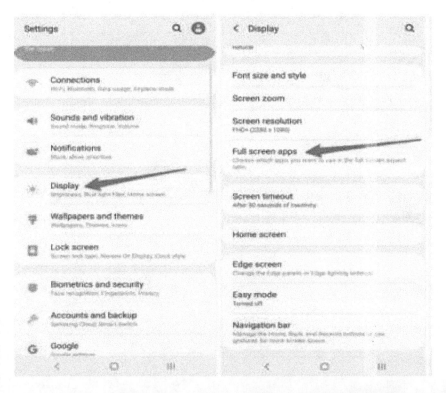

- Then toggle on the switch for **Hide Front Camera**

- A little black bar will now appear at the top of your screen to cover the front camera

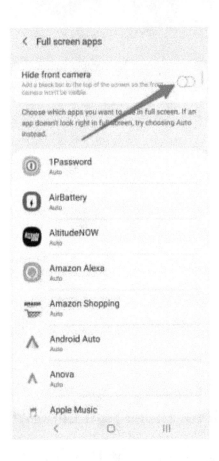

Take Photos with Palm

You can also take photos on your device without clicking the shutter button. Once you show your palm to the camera, it will automatically take photos. This is especially useful for times you are unable to reach the shutter button but can show your palm to the camera. To enable this feature,

- Go to the camera app

- Click on the camera settings

- Tap **Shooting methods**

- Now toggle on the option for **Show Palm**

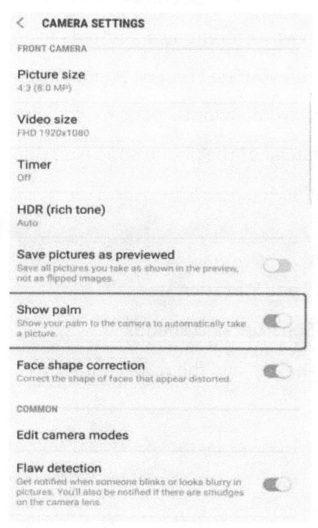

Chapter 11: Audio Experience

Play with Sound Settings (Separate App Sounds)

The Galaxy S20 series has another exciting feature known as the Separate App Sounds. This feature allows you to have two different audio outputs from two different apps on your device. For example, you can choose to play your favorite podcast on your wireless speaker instead of the phone's speaker. And it is very easy to set up too.

- Go to settings
- Click on **Sound and Vibration**
- Now click on **Separate App Sounds**
- Then choose the app and the sound output you want
- That's all!

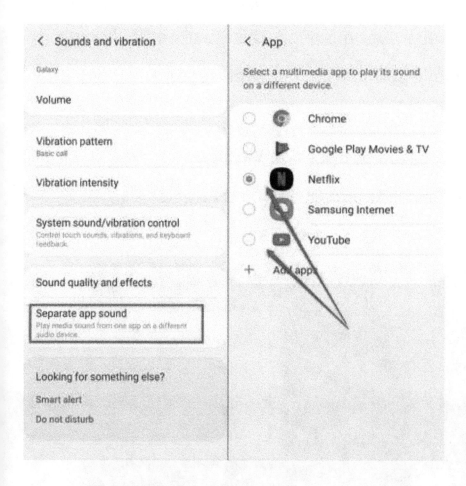

Customize Sound Based on Age

The Samsung Galaxy S20 series allows tailoring sounds from your phone to suit your age and preference. The S20 comes with built-in capabilities to tweak the high and low tones to suit your listening preferences. Enabling this feature will help you hear well-detailed and more defined sounds that may otherwise be missing. This feature is known as Adaptive Sound. To enable this feature,

- Go to settings
- Click on **Sounds and Vibrations**
- Select **Sound Quality and Effects**
- Then click on **Adapt Sound**

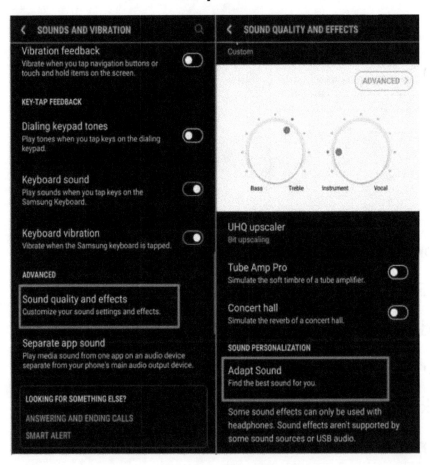

- Create a custom sound profile or choose a readymade profile for your age
- To create a custom sound profile, click on the **Add Personalized sound** button at the end of your screen
- Plug-in your earphones and your device will walk you through the process.
- On your screen, you will see the real-time changes in the equalizer
- Save the settings once done
- Tap the cog icon if you want to hear the difference between the two profiles

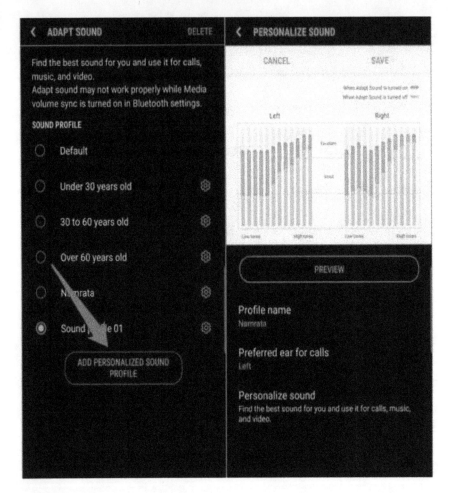

Dolby Atmos

This feature helps to enhance your audio experience by increasing the default volume of your phone by about twenty-five percent while adding special effects at the same time. Another cool thing about this feature is that it has three more profiles for Music, Voices, and Movie.

With the music profile enabled, you will enjoy a clean and rich sound experience while the Voice profile enhances voices in movies or videos, and the Movie profile gives you an immersive experience.

This feature is disabled by default. To enable Dolby Atmos,

- Go to settings
- Click on **Sounds and vibration**
- Tap **Advanced sound settings**
- Click on **Sound Quality and Effects**
- Enable **Dolby Atmos** by moving the switch to the right
- To change the sound profile, click on **Dolby Atmos** and select your preference on the next screen

Using UHQ Upscaler

Just like the Dolby Atmos, your phone has dedicated profiles for earphones. When listening to songs on your phone, you can switch between Concert Hall, Tube Amp Pro, and UHQ Upscaler sound setting. UHQ Upscaler comes with DSD and UHQ 32-bit support to ensure that you enjoy higher quality audio.

- Go to settings
- Click on **Sounds and Vibration**
- Tap **Advanced Sound Settings**
- Click on **Sound Quality and Effects**
- Scroll down on the page and click on **UHQ Upscaler**
- On the next screen, click on your choice from the two options displayed

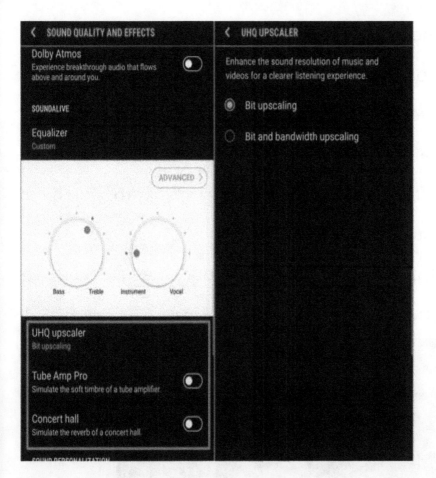

Change Bluetooth Audio Codec

Your Samsung S20 supports several Bluetooth audio codecs like LDAC, aptX, etc. So, if you have a pair of LDAC or aptX HD headphones, you can switch to the profile which your headphones support. But to enjoy this feature, you need to enable the option from the Developer settings on your device.

To unlock the Developer settings

- Go to settings

- Click on **About phone**

- Tap **Software Information** seven times

- After doing this, use the search bar to search for **Bluetooth Audio Codec**

- A pop-up will display on your screen, change to your choice

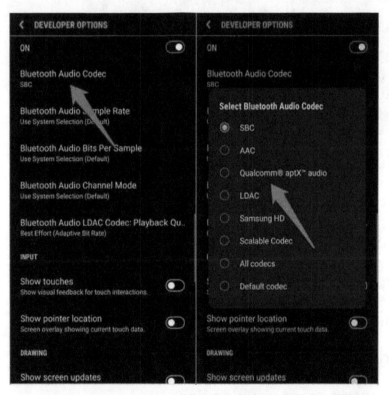

Turn Off Unnecessary Sounds

Your Samsung S20 is set by default to make little noises for every time you touch it and this can be pretty annoying both for the user and everyone else around you. These extra noises and vibration will also drain your battery faster. To turn off this noise.

- Go to settings

- Click on **Sounds and vibration**

- Tap **System Sounds and Vibrations**

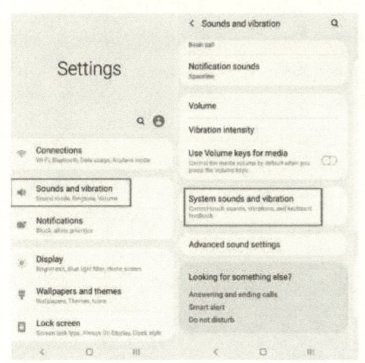

- Then switch off every sound that you do not need.

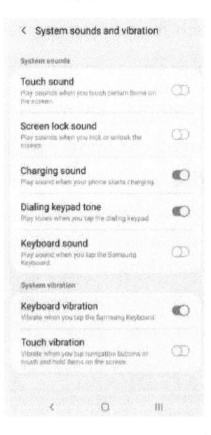

Chapter 12: Explore the Sound Assistant App

The Sound Assistant app is an in-house app designed to tweak the system sounds, and it comes packed with several features. One advantage of this app is the floating audio button that lets you access the sound settings quickly. To enable the sound profiles or set the floating equalizer, all you need to do is click on the button to activate a floating window. Then click on the Settings icon, and you will find all you need. To enable the floating button,

- Launch the Sound Assistant app
- Toggle on the switch for Floating button
- Click on the card to set how long you want the button to remain on the home screen
- Then hit any of the volume rocker buttons to see the floating window

Increase Volume Step

You may have been in a situation where you need to adjust the volume of your device just a little. But when you tap the volume key up, the speakers blast louder than you want. The default Samsung volume steps are 15, which most users are okay with. But for users who do not fancy the Samsung default volume steps, you can try the Volume Steps feature.

To activate this feature,

- Go to the Advanced settings of the SoundAssistant app.

- Drag the slider for step volume to your preferred number

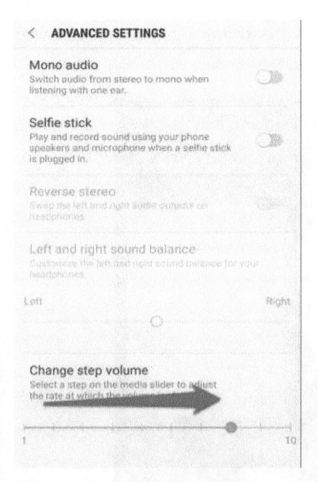

Save and Share EQ Settings

Your device allows you to share your equalizer settings with friends, thanks to the SoundAssistant app. To do this,

- Bring up the floating equalizer window for the SoundAssistant app

- Adjust your settings as desired and save it

166

- Then click on the share icon to share with friends.

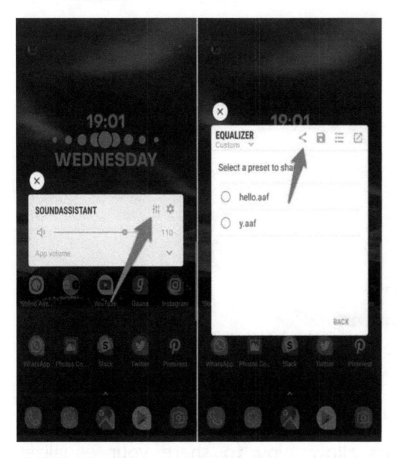

Manage Volume for Individual Apps

Again, the SoundAssistant app helps you to assign individual volume to several multimedia apps. With this feature, you can increase the volume for YouTube videos to the highest while keeping that of Google Music at 5%.

The first step is to add the apps

- Launch the SoundAssistant app
- Select individual app volume options
- Add the apps and modify the volume to your preference.
- When next you launch the modified apps, the volume will revert to the one you set in the SoundAssistant app.

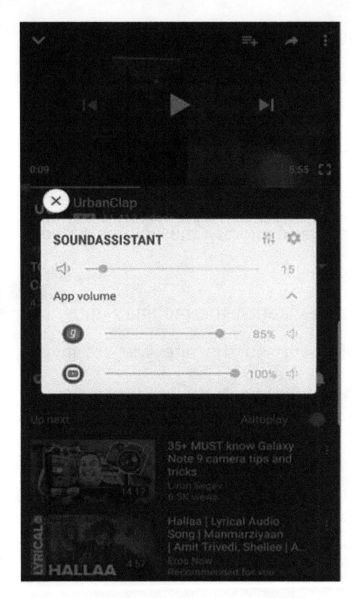

- To decrease or increase the volume for an app, launch the SoundAssitant floating window, click on the Arrow icon and pull the slider for each of the apps

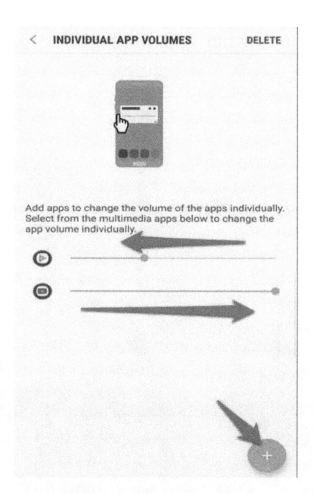

Add apps to change the volume of the apps individually.
Select from the multimedia apps below to change the
app volume individually.

Personalize Sound Profiles

The key feature of the SoundAssistant app is to personalize sound profiles as it allows you to set individual volume levels for different times in a day. For example, you can set your phone to be on silent mode at 8 a.m once you enter the office and revert to normal mode at 6 p.m. to do this,

- Launch the SoundAssistant app

- Click on **Scenarios**

- Edit as you want

- Click on **Save** once done

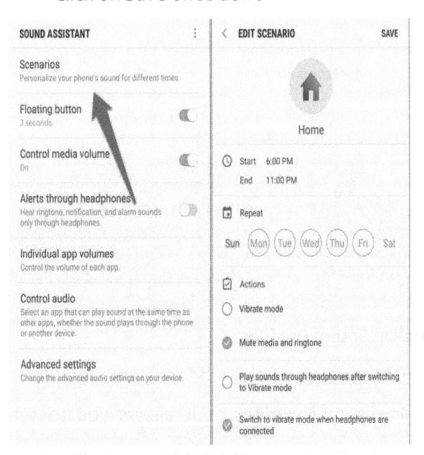

Chapter 13: Device Security

In-Display Ultrasonic Fingerprint Scanner

The S20 comes with an in-display ultrasonic fingerprint scanner that is accurate and fast. To unlock your smartphone, simply place your thumb on the lock screen. The S20 requires every owner to use the ultrasonic fingerprint scanner. The steps below will guide you on how to set up the fingerprint lock

- Go to **Settings**
- Click on **Biometrics and Security**
- Select **Fingerprints**
- Now click on **Add Fingerprints** and set up your fingerprint

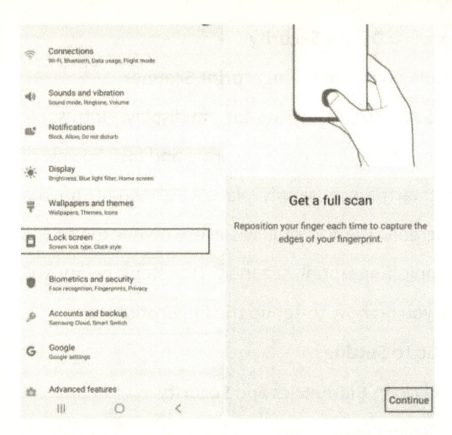

🛜	**Connections**	
	Wi-Fi, Bluetooth, Data usage, Flight mode	
🔊	**Sounds and vibration**	
	Sound mode, Ringtone, Volume	
🔔	**Notifications**	
	Block, Allow, Do not disturb	
🔆	**Display**	
	Brightness, Blue light filter, Home screen	
🎨	**Wallpapers and themes**	
	Wallpapers, Themes, Icons	
🔒	**Lock screen**	
	Screen lock type, Clock style	
🛡	**Biometrics and security**	
	Face recognition, Fingerprints, Privacy	
🔑	**Accounts and backup**	
	Samsung Cloud, Smart Switch	
G	**Google**	
	Google settings	
⚙	**Advanced features**	

Get a full scan

Reposition your finger each time to capture the edges of your fingerprint.

Continue

Enable Fingerprint Icon

The in-display fingerprint scanner is one of the coolest features in the S20. It is not only fast but also accurate. But one problem with this scanner is that it is easy to miss it, mainly when the display is off. In cases like this, your best bet is to activate the Fingerprint scanner icon. The S20 makes the icon visible when you tap your phone screen, even when the screen is off. To enable this feature,

- Go to settings
- Click on **Biometrics and Security**
- Select **Fingerprints**
- Move the switch beside **'Show icon when the screen is off'** to the right to enable it
- You can disable this option once you can tell its location.
- To unlock your phone, tap once on your device screen, then press your thumb against the screen

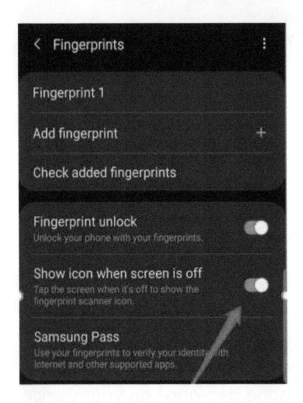

The Alternate Look Feature

It's 2020! Several phone users are familiar with the face recognition feature that unlocks a locked screen in seconds. Yet, there are still some glitches with using this feature when you put on accessories like wearing dark-tinted sunglasses.

Samsung's One UI 2,0 has addressed this issue with the new Alternate Look feature. With this feature enabled, your phone will recognize you even with accessories on. To activate this feature,

- Go to settings
- Click on **Biometric and Security**
- Click on **Face recognition**
- Then click on **Add Alternative Look**

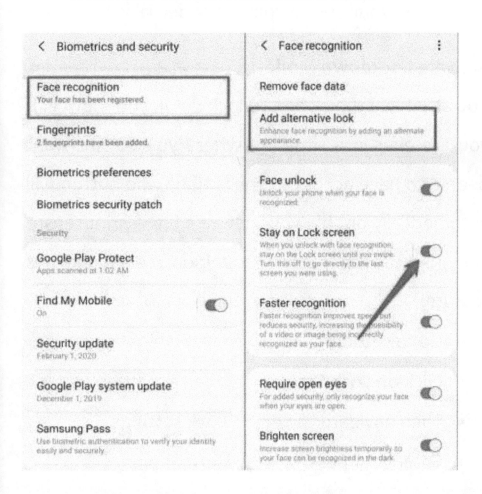

- Now run a dry test to confirm that it's working.

- You can also activate the 'Stay on Lock Screen' option on this same screen. This option configures your phone to remain on the lock screen after you unlock the phone. This will help prevent misdialing or accidental app launches when your phone unlock accidentally.

Activate Lockdown Mode

You also have the option to lock down your device. If you are ever in a situation where you do not want people to have access to your phone, the button will automatically disable your device's fingerprint sensor and Iris scanner/ facial recognition. To enable this feature,

- Go to settings
- Click on **Lock Screen**
- Then navigate to **Secure Lock settings**
- Enter your password, pattern or pin

- You will now see the option for **Show Lockdown**

- Activate the **Lockdown Mode**

You have now activated the Lockdown Mode. To use this feature, press and hold down the power button until you get some options displayed on your screen. Now click on **Lockdown** to secure your phone from third-party.

Note: once you activate the Lockdown mode, you have automatically turned off notifications, biometrics unlock, and smart lock on the Lock Screen.

Hide Sensitive Apps

Smartphones are not just to make calls and send messages as you can now do more with your smartphone. Some of the apps we use contain sensitive and personal information that we want to keep secret. The steps below will guide you on how to

hide apps on your Samsung S20:

- Long-press on a blank space on the home screen

- Then click on **Home Screen Settings**

- Scroll down and click on **Hide Apps**

- Choose the apps you want to hide and click on

  Apply

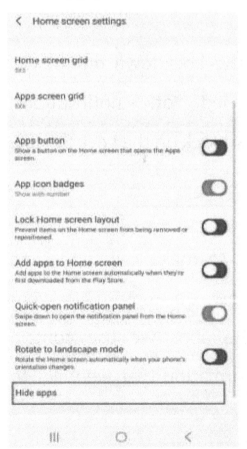

How to Unhide Apps

- Long-press on a blank space on the home screen
- Then click on **Home Screen Settings**
- Scroll down and click on **Hide Apps**
- Click on the minus (-) sign beside hidden apps at the top of your screen.
- Once done, click on **Apply.**

Hide Albums in Gallery

Another cool feature of the S20 series is being able to hide your albums and photos in the Gallery, especially if you have private videos and pictures you do not want others to view. To use this feature,

- Open the gallery app
- Click on the 3-dot icon at the top right corner of your screen
- Click on **Hide or Unhide**
- Now choose the albums you want to hide.

- Once done, you will no longer see the selected albums in the gallery until you disable this feature.

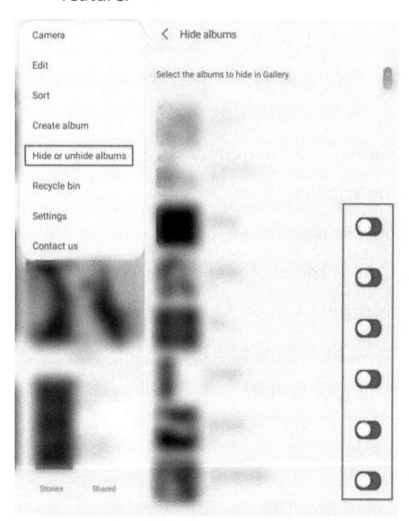

Secured Folder

This feature is used to protect specified emails, photos, contacts, or apps from third-party access. It serves as another layer of security. Follow the steps below to create your secure folder

- Go to **Settings**
- Click on **Biometrics and security**
- Tap **Secure Folder**

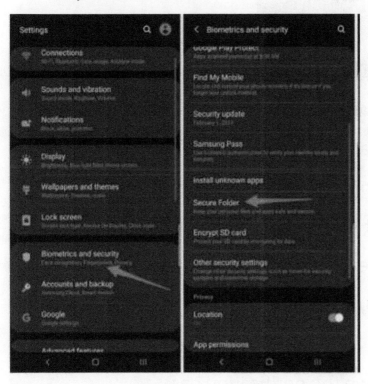

- Then follow the prompts to set up your secure folder successfully

Hide Sensitive Files with Secured Folder

We all have a sensitive file we do not want others to see, an odd photo we want to keep private or an app or game that we do not want another person to view on our phone. Samsung allows you to hide these files with the Secure Folder. Follow the steps below to use this feature

- Pull down the notification bar.

- Click on the **Secure Folder** icon

- Agree to the terms and conditions then proceed to set up a Samsung account, if you don't have one already.

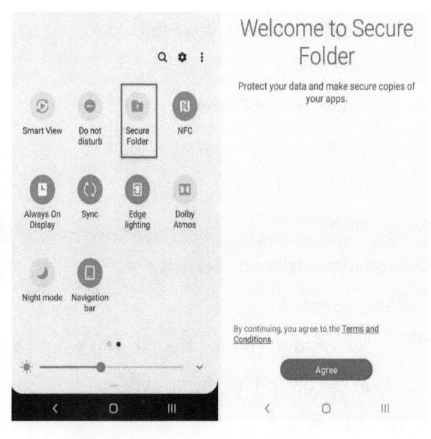

- After signing in successfully, you will have a secure folder that you can only access with your fingerprint, pattern, password, or PIN.

- Proceed to add individual files and apps to the secure folder.

Follow the steps below to hide the secure folder:

- Go to **Settings**

- Click on **Biometrics and Security**

- Tap **Secure Folder**

- Click on **Hide Secure Folder**

- Then tap **OK**

To access your hidden folder,

- Go to settings

- Click on **Biometrics and Security**

- Tap **Secure Folder**

- Then click on the icon for the file you want to access at the bottom of the screen

Find My Mobile

Samsung has the 'Find My Mobile' service on all Galaxy devices. To access the setting,

- Go to the settings app

- Click on **Biometrics and security**

- Then click on **Find My Mobile**

- Feel free to adjust the settings to your preference

- If you ever lose your phone, visit findmymobile.samsung.com, input your Samsung login details to access your Samsung account, and control or track down a lost phone.

Chapter 14: Manage Your Notification Settings

To quickly access your settings, notifications and more, open the notification panel

Quick settings

Device settings

View all

Notification cards

View the Notification panel

To access the notification panel from anywhere on your phone,

- Drag down the status bar to display the notification panel

- Swipe further down to see your notification details

- Click on an item to open it

- Drag a notification to the right or left to clear a single notification

- Click on the notification settings to customize notifications

- Close the notification panel by clicking the Back key or dragging upward from the bottom of your screen.

Customize Your Quick Settings

To easily access your quick settings, simply swipe down from the top of your screen. But, you may not be satisfied with the default lineup and may prefer to customize to your liking. To do this,

- Click on the three vertical dots located at the top right of the notification bar screen.

- Click on **Button Order**

- Select what you want to add to the view

- Then arrange them in a position that suits your preference (for faster access).

- In the same view as the Button Order, click on **Status Bar** to modify the settings and enable functions like turning on battery percentage

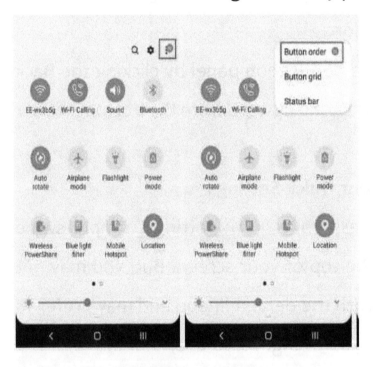

Touch and Hold to See Notifications

You can change the way notifications are displayed on your device. To do this

- Go to the home screen and long-press on any blank part of the screen

- Click on **Home Screen Settings**

- Select **App icon badges**

- Scroll down on the screen and move the switch beside **Show notifications** to the right to enable

- Once this feature is enabled, whenever you touch and hold down on an icon in the app drawer or on the home screen, unread notifications will show in a pop-up window for you to quickly check them without having to open the app

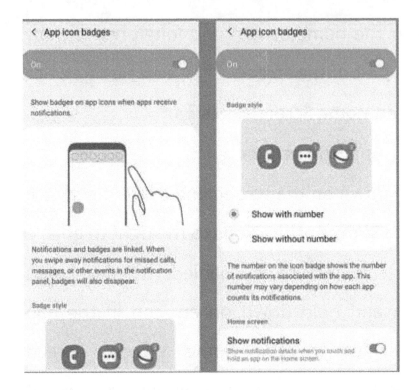

Snooze alerts

The settings below will guide you on how to remove alerts from the notification shade for a defined period by snoozing them.

- Slowly swipe left or right on an alert until a bell and a settings icon appear
- Click on the bell

- Choose from the amount of time listed on the next screen to snooze the alert

Set Notification Reminders

Are you aware that your phone can send you reminders to check missed notifications for specific apps? To activate this,

- Go to the settings app
- Search for **Notification Reminder** in the search bar
- Click on **Remind Every** and choose your preferred time interval
- Then, navigate to **Selected Reminders** section and move the switch to the right for all the apps that you want

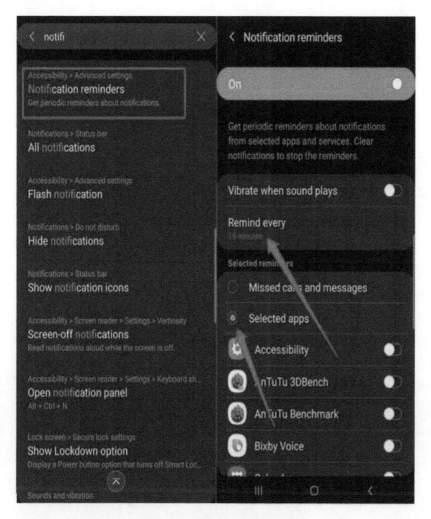

Enable Flashlight Notifications

This feature is particularly helpful when you are in a dark environment, movie theatre, or when your phone is in silent mode. This feature flashes the LED to notify you of incoming calls and messages. To enable this feature,

- Go to settings. Click on **Accessibility**

- Select **Advanced settings**

- Click on **Flashlight notification**

- Now toggle on the option for **Screen flash** and **Camera flash**

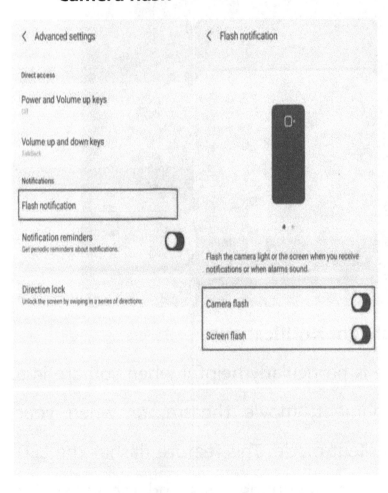

Chapter 15: Wi-fi Calling

Enable Wi-Fi Calling on the Galaxy S20

Wi-fi calling uses your home Wi-fi network rather than your cell phone signals to make calls. This is mostly for times when the cellular signals are bad. The added bonus to this is that you get to enjoy higher call quality. This is how to enable it on your S20

- Go to settings
- Click on **Connections**
- Now toggle on the switch for **Wi-Fi calling**

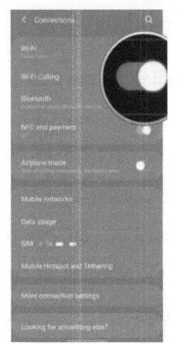

Enable Wifi Calling from the S20 Dialer

If you are unable to see the Wi-fi calling toggle under your phone settings, you can enable it directly from the phone dialer.

- Open the dialer from your home screen
- Click on the overflow menu, that is, the three vertical dots on the right
- Select **Settings**
- Then toggle on **Wi-fi calling**

- You can now begin to enjoy the smoothness of Wi-fi calling

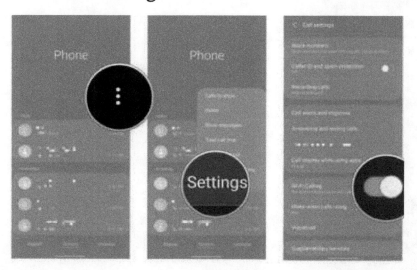

Using the Google Duo in the Phone Dialer

Samsung integrated the Google Duo directly into the dialer for the S20 series so that you can easily make video calls with family and friends. Here's a guide on how to make Duo calls

- Open the phone dialer

- Choose the contact you want to video call

- Click on the Duo icon under the contact's details to begin a video call

- Your video call will now be transferred over to Duo.

- You can also move from a regular voice call to a video call. To do this while on a voice call, click on the video call button to switch to Duo video call.

Chapter 16: Maximizing Display on the Galaxy S20

Always On Display

This beautiful feature gives your phone a super chic look while displaying notifications, weather info, battery percentage, and time. You can also add stylish watch faces to display above it. To enable this feature,

- Go to settings
- Click on **Lock Screen**
- Navigate to **Always On Display** and move the switch to the right to activate
- You can customize it further by tapping on the card and selecting **Display Mode.**
- Then click on **Show Always**

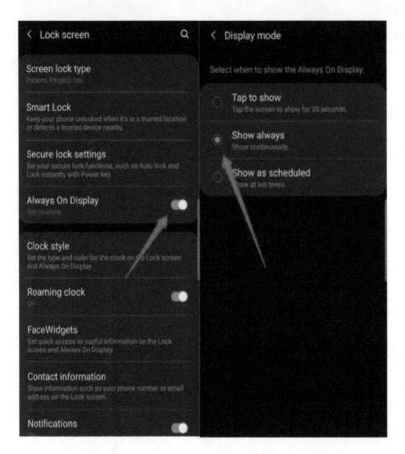

- Then return to the **Lock Screen** page and click on **Clock Style**

- Click on **Always-on Display,** and you will see various options to choose from

- Pick the one you like and tap the **Done** button

- Lock your phone and see the beautiful display come alive

Note: You can also change the color of the Clock Faces. To do this, simply click on **Color** under **Clock Style** and choose your preferred color.

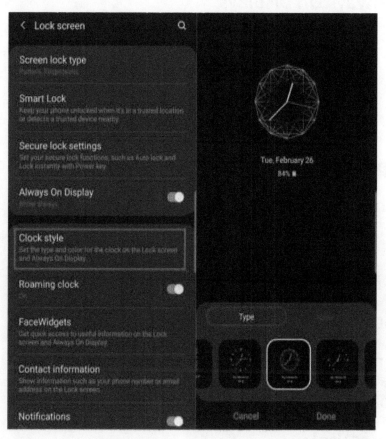

Always on Display (AOD) Themes

Use custom themes for AOD.

- Go to the home screen and long-press on any blank part of the screen

- Click on **Themes** ⌐ . Select **AODs**

- Click on an AOD to preview and download to '**My Always On Displays**'

- To view all your downloaded AODs, click on **My Page** 👤

- Then choose the one you want to use and click on **Apply**

Max Out the Display Resolution

The S20 display isn't automatically set at the maximum resolution in a bid to save battery life. But, setting your phone to the maximum resolution will help you enjoy some sharpness on your device.

- Go to the settings app

- Click on **Display**

- Select **Screen Resolution**

- Choose your preferred resolution. The maximum is 3040 by 1440 pixels

Screen brightness

Adjust your screen brightness to suit your personal preferences or lighting condition.

- Go to settings

- Click on **Display**

- On the next screen, drag the slider under **Brightness** to your desired settings

- Click on **Adaptive brightness** to automatically adjust the brightness of your screen based on the current lighting conditions

Change Refresh Rate

One of the major highlights of the newest additions to the Samsung family is the 120Hz refresh rate screen. This rate makes daily interactions to be smooth. By default, the refresh rate is set to 60Hz, but you can switch to 120Hz with the steps below

- Go to settings

- Click on **Display** ☀

- Select **Motion smoothness**

- Click on **High refresh rate (120Hz)** to convert to the 120Hz mode

- Then click on **Apply** to confirm the changes

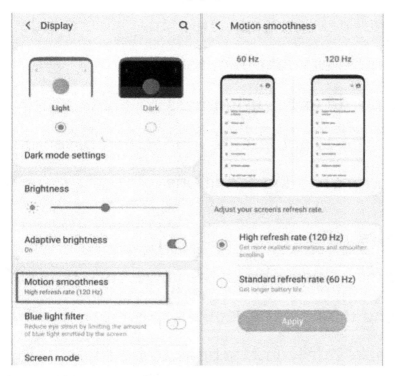

Note: the 120Hz mode uses up your battery faster because the screen is effectively refreshing twice as quickly as usual.

Screen mode

Your phone has several screen mode options that you can adjust to meet different situations for screen quality. Feel free to choose the mode that suits you.

- Go to settings

- Click on **Display**

- Click on **Screen Mode** and choose from the different screen modes displayed on your screen.

Blue light filter

This feature, particularly for those that operate their phone at night, helps you to sleep better. You can set up a schedule to automatically enable or disable this feature

- Go to settings. Click on **Display**

- Click on **Blue light filter** and choose from the displayed option

1. Click **Turn On Now** to enable the feature

2. Pull the opacity slider to set the opacity of the filter

3. Click on **Turn on as scheduled** to create a schedule for when the feature should be enabled. You can choose either the **Custom schedule** or **Sunset to sunrise.**

Enable One-Handed Mode

One of the first options you should enable on your phone is the conventional one-handed mode. With this option, you can either swipe up diagonally from the corners of the home screen or tap three times on the home screen to shrink the screen, thereby making it easy to work. This mode is most useful when typing or using your phone in a crowded environment. But you have to activate the feature manually using the steps below:

- Go to Finder and type 'one-handed' in the search bar

- Click on the settings card as shown in the screenshot below

- Now toggle the switch for **One-handed mode**

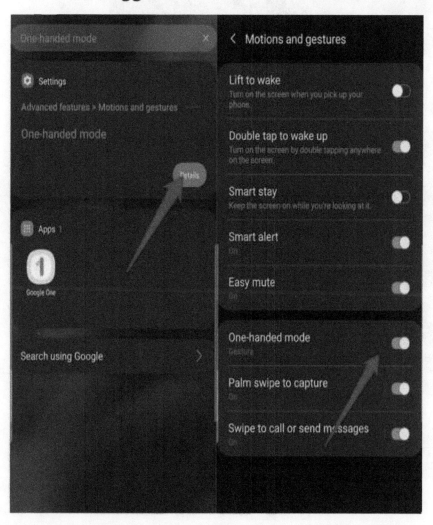

Another way to activate this feature is

- Go to settings

- Click on **Motions and gestures**

- Now select between Button or Gesture

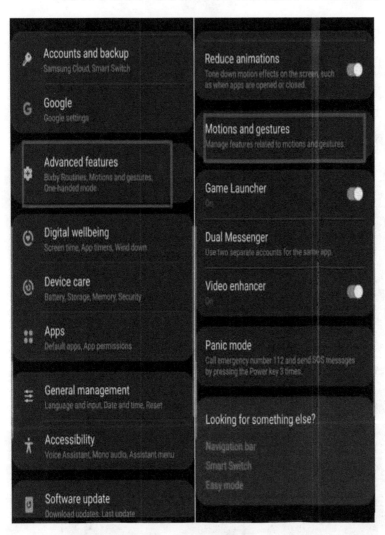

One-Hand Operation + App

This app was designed by Samsung to customize the navigation gestures further and is particularly useful for users who find it challenging to get to the bottom half of their device. It comes with two customizable handles on both sides of the device and allows you to perform functions like launching the previous app, going back, and opening recent menus just by swiping any of the handles. You can customize these handles to your taste. For now, each of the handles supports three gestures: horizontal, diagonal down, and diagonal up.

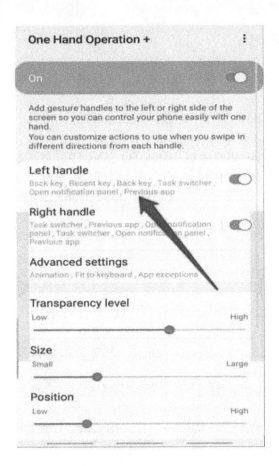

To set the gestures,

- Click on a handle and add your desired action

- You can also add Long Swipe gestures and then customize it

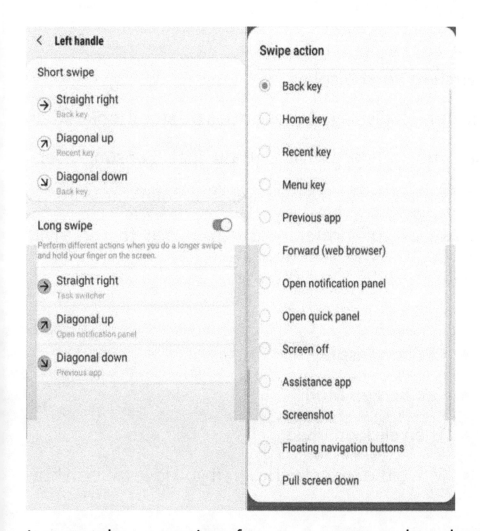

It may take some time for you to get used to these new gestures, but once you familiarize yourself with them, you will enjoy navigating the screen of your S20. **Cool tip:** you can have the Edge screen on one edge and the One Hand Operation+ on the other edge, depending on your preference and convenience.

Switch to Vivid Display

The default display of the S20 has a natural look rather than the standard Vivid setting that Samsung users are familiar with. If you think the colors are not as intense as you prefer, you can switch to the Vivid display with the steps below

- Go to settings
- Click on **Display**
- Tap **Screen Mode**
- Then click on **Vivid**
- Move the slider to the left if you love a bluish hue

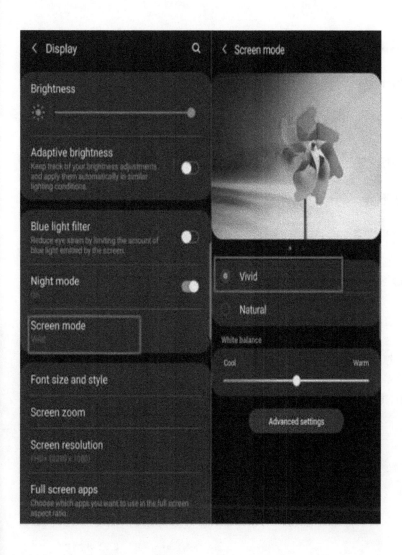

Chapter 17: Advanced Features of the S20

Dual Messenger

Most recent apps now have the Dual Messenger feature. This feature allows you to use more than one account of the same app like Snapchat or WhatsApp. To enable this feature,

- Go to settings
- Click on **Advanced features**
- Select **Dual Messenger** and toggle on the option for all the apps you want to clone.

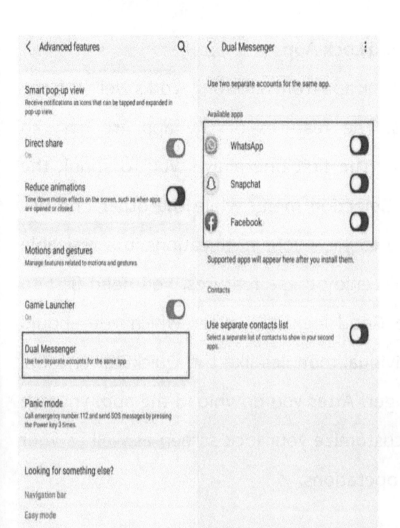

< Advanced features   Q

Smart pop-up view
Receive notifications as icons that can be tapped and expanded in pop-up view.

Direct share
On

Reduce animations
Tone down motion effects on the screen, such as when apps are opened or closed.

Motions and gestures
Manage features related to motions and gestures.

Game Launcher
On

Dual Messenger
Use two separate accounts for the same app

Panic mode
Call emergency number 112 and send SOS messages by pressing the Power key 3 times.

Looking for something else?

Navigation bar

Easy mode

< Dual Messenger   ⋮

Use two separate accounts for the same app.

Available apps

WhatsApp

Snapchat

Facebook

Supported apps will appear here after you install them.

Contacts

Use separate contacts list
Select a separate list of contacts to show in your second apps.

Get the Good Lock App

The Good Lock app from Samsung works well with the S20 series. The features of the app are easy to understand. The first one allows you to shrink the **Overview Selection menu** while the other one will enable you to view your notifications in a resizable window. To enjoy these features, you need first to install the Good lock app, after which you should install individual modules like the QuickStar and the Task Changer. After you download the app, you can use it to customize your lock screen as well as your one-hand operations.

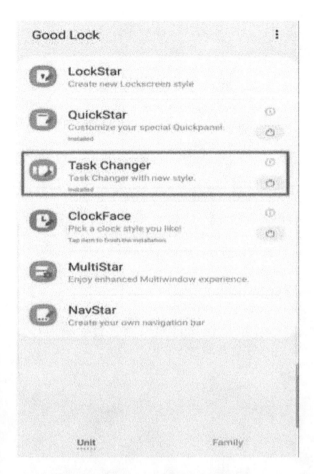

LockStar
Create new Lockscreen style

QuickStar
Customize your special Quickpanel
Installed

Task Changer
Task Changer with new style.
Installed

ClockFace
Pick a clock style you like!
Tap item to finish the installation

MultiStar
Enjoy enhanced Multiwindow experience.

NavStar
Create your own navigation bar

Unit   Family

To activate the Mini mode,

- Open the Good lock app.

- Click on **Task Changer,** toggle on the option.

- Then toggle on the switch for Mini Mode

- On the same screen, you may also want to explore the different layout types.

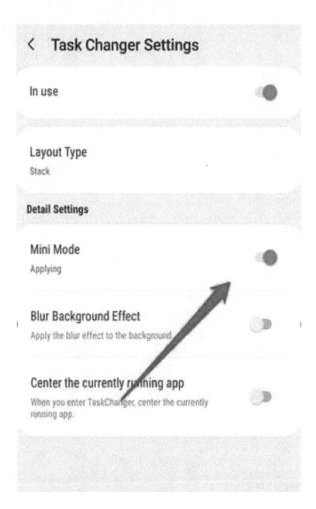

- Go back to the home screen of the app

- Click on **QuickStar** and toggle on the option

- Then enable the Notification Popup Button.

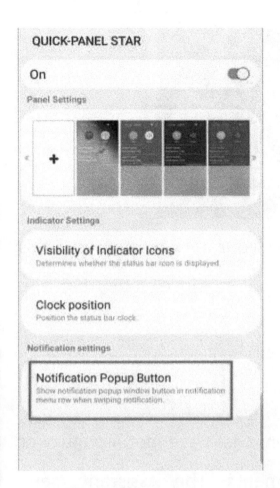

QUICK-PANEL STAR

On

Panel Settings

Indicator Settings

Visibility of Indicator Icons
Determines whether the status bar icon is displayed.

Clock position
Position the status bar clock.

Notification settings

Notification Popup Button
Show notification popup window button in notification menu row when swiping notification.

- Once activated, you will see a button displayed in the notification bubble. Once you click on it, it will automatically open your notifications in a resizable window.

Note: Not all apps on your device supports this feature. Instagram does not support it, but Whatsapp does.

Assistant Menu

This feature is for persons that have motor control or other physical impairments. The Assistant menu allows you to access hardware buttons and other parts of the screen just by swiping or typing. Follow the steps below to activate this feature

- Go to settings
- Click on **Accessibility**
- Then click on **Interaction and Dexterity**

- Now enable the **Assistant Menu** option

- The Assistant menu will appear on your screen. You can drag it to any part of the screen that you want.

- Click on the menu button to access options like the Screen off, back button, Volume, Home button, Screenshots, Recents button, and so on.

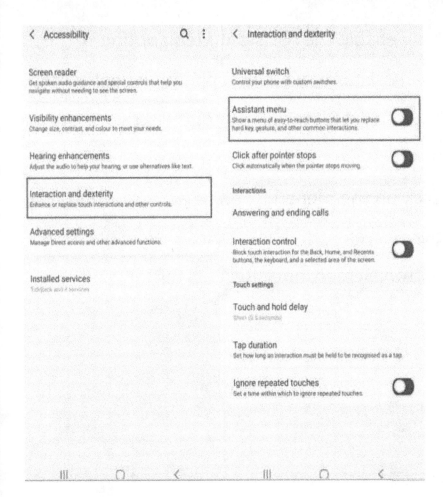

Pin Windows Feature

This feature basically means launching an app and pinning the app to your screen so that you do not accidentally close the app. Note that when an app is pinned, you will be unable to use other features outside the app, calls, and messages will also be blocked. To activate this feature,

- Go to settings
- Click on **Biometrics and security**
- Select **Other Security settings**
- Then enable the option for **Pin windows**

Once you have enabled this feature, you can begin to pin any app. To pin an app,

- Launch the app as normal
- Then press the recent app button
- Click on the app icon located at the top of your screen
- Then select **Pin this app.**

To close the pinned app

- Press and hold simmer down until you see the recent apps and back soft button.
- Click on it to close

Using Pop-up View

This feature is a smart option that permits some specific apps to pop-up on top of other apps. This is similar to how Facebook Messenger operates. When this feature is active, any new message that comes into your phone comes as a round pop-up icon that you can click on to launch the messaging app. This feature can only be used with apps that support multi-window.

To activate this feature

- Go to settings
- Click on **Advanced features**
- Click on **Smart pop-up view**
- Remember to toggle on only apps that support multi-window. However, this feature is best for messaging apps

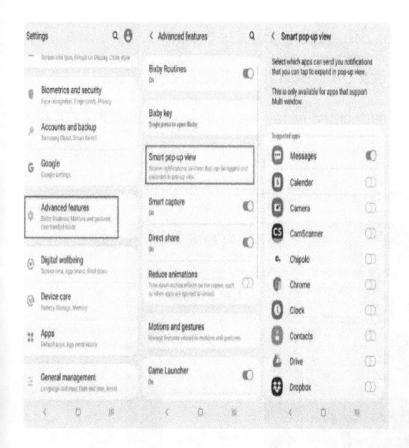

Split-screen apps

Your device allows you to use more than one app per time. To do this,

- Navigate to the multitasking view and look for any of the apps you want to access in the split-screen mode

- Click on the app's icon

- Then click on **Open in Split-Screen View**

- The first app you launch will automatically minimize to the top of the screen until you launch the second app

www.ingramcontent.com/pod-product-compliance
Lightning Source LLC
LaVergne TN
LVHW041210050326
832903LV00021B/554